THE CHALLENGE
OF
WRECK
FISHING

THE CHALLENGE

— OF —

WRECK FISHING

LINDSEY GREEN

BLANDFORD

A BLANDFORD BOOK

First published in the UK 1993
by Blandford
(a Cassell imprint)
Villiers House
41/47 Strand
LONDON
WC2N 5JE

Distributed in the United States by Sterling Publishing Co., Inc.
387 Park Avenue South, New York, NY 10016–8810

Distributed in Australia by Capricorn Link (Australia) Pty Ltd
P.O. Box 665, Lane Cove, NSW 2066

British Library Cataloguing-in-Publication Data
A catalogue record for this book is available from the British Library.

ISBN 0-7137-2337-8

Typeset by MS Filmsetting Limited, Frome, Somerset

Printed and bound in Great Britain

CONTENTS

I dedicate this book to the ladies of my family: my wife, Julie; my mother, Dorothy Leah Green; and in fond memory of Maureen Cooper, whose quiet courage filled all of us with pride.

ACKNOWLEDGEMENTS

I would like to thank all the people who contributed their valuable time and practical assistance while I was researching *The Challenge of Wreck Fishing*. In particular I would like to thank both Dianne Sollis of DAM (UK) Ltd — a lady with a terrific sense of humour — for the many kindnesses towards both myself and the disabled anglers with whom I have been working, and Chris Leibbrandt of Ryobi Tackle, whose assistance was invaluable, especially where it helped one particular disabled angler to catch the biggest fish of his life.

I would also like to thank:

Stephen McCaveny of Daiwa Tackle;

Sharon Davies of Shimano;

Alan Stevens, skipper of the Torquay-based charter-boat *Striker*, who volunteered photographs and practical assistance to both myself and disabled anglers of my acquaintance;

Ken Hatsell, especially for the photographs he kindly contributed;

Tom Burness of Titan Manufacturing.

Lastly, it gives me great pleasure to introduce the underwater photography of Diana Ingram. In hearing of this project, she kindly volunteered some of the best underwater shots that it has been my privilege to see. Not only that, but in her subsequent exploration of several wrecks she was able to provide some valuable insights into their inhabitants and the environment itself. For these and her other efforts on my behalf, I would like to express my sincere gratitude and extend my best wishes for her future career.

Lindsey Green

INTRODUCING THE WRECK

It was 10 August 1918, a time of great apprehension for the hardy souls who ventured to sea in waters that had been declared safe, swept clear of the danger of mines. This statement was easy to make but failed to allay the lingering, nagging doubts that must inevitably have remained in almost every sailor's mind. On a clear day, those doubts must have been enough to prompt a very sharp lookout, but on this particular day the danger was multiplied many times by the thick fog that had descended on the *Bretagne* as she moved slowly eastward.

In her prime, the *Bretagne* must have presented a picture fit to move any artist to reach for his brushes: a tall, schooner-rigged steamer of 1,439 tons (1,462 tonnes), perhaps a trifle dusty from the nearly 2,000 tons (2,032 tonnes) of coal that were buried in her holds, but still picturesque as she cut through the morning fog on her journey from Barry to Rouen.

By a strange quirk of fate, when disaster struck, it was not in the shape of a mine, but in the looming form of the French steamer, the *Renée Marthe*, which appeared out of the fog and dealt the *Bretagne* such a blow on the starboard side that her steering gear jammed and she quickly began to take on water. The bows of the *Renée Marthe* crumpled, but she was still able to limp into Dartmouth. The *Bretagne* was not as lucky, even though a fishing trawler appeared and managed to remove most of her crew safely and then take her in tow.

Back on board the *Bretagne*, three men (her Captain, J. W. Johannesson; the first mate, Harry Watterson; and Dick Pym, a naval gunner) struggled to free the steering gear, trying desperately to make the steamer easier to tow. Their efforts were to no avail. Ultimately they were forced to abandon ship as the water lapped dangerously over the deck itself. Tragically, it was then that Harry Watterson made a fatal mistake. As he dived below to retrieve his personal belongings from his cabin, a wave slammed the outer door shut and the *Bretagne* nose-dived to the bottom, where she came to rest in some 80 ft (25 m) of water.

Over the years that followed, the *Bretagne* was to see many changes in both her own condition and the environment into which she had settled. A bewildering assortment of small creatures came to take refuge in the shelter that she afforded, whilst sponges and a proliferation of marine vegetation, barnacles and shellfish swiftly covered her rusting hulk, both increasing the cover that she offered and making their own contribution to the food chain. Shoals of small fish hunted frantically for food, or hid when they themselves were threatened by the larger fish that came to hunt through, around and above the wreck itself. Congers, perhaps a few at first, then in greater numbers, took up residence both within the hull and wherever they could find a lair. Huge shoals of mackerel wheeled above the decks, in turn bringing ling, pollack, coalfish and the occasional shark, while vast numbers of sand-eels, in season, swarmed around the hull and attracted still other predators to the wreck.

Huge prawns and a variety of crabs and molluscs began to exert their own appeal, drawing colourful wrasse away from their regular haunts and tempting them into making the *Bretagne* their permanent home. Red and black bream came and went in season, while dogfish, flatfish and pout began to inhabit the wreck and the surrounding area in ever-increasing numbers. Even bass came to regard the wreck as a stopover station — a roadside diner — along the path of their migratory treks, where they could feed heavily upon the vast accumulation of food before carrying on with their pre-destined journeys.

Those species such as flatfish, which prefer to live on sandy ground, found that a large sandbank began to build up against the part of the ship which was facing the tide, whilst a scour, a depression created by the removal of sand, began to form at the opposite quarter. Here larger fish, such as turbot, angler-fish and rays, came to prey upon the smaller fish which were themselves attracted by the litter of food that surrounded the wreck. Meanwhile, just past the scour, floating particles, remnants from the congers' meals and other bits and pieces, drifted downtide to draw scavengers such as dogfish and pout, and still more crabs, which in turn attracted smooth-hounds, rays and cuttlefish, both to investigate and then to

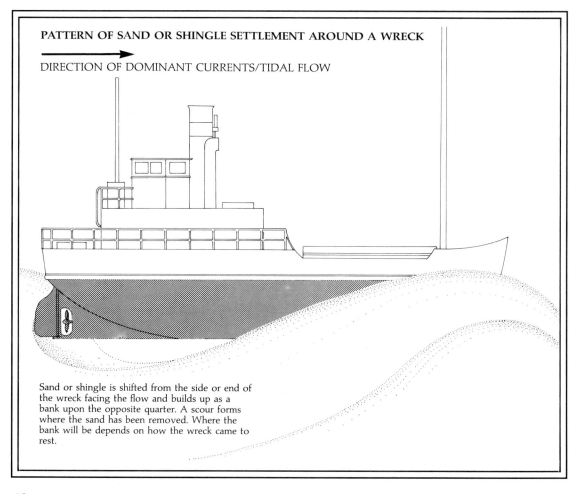

PATTERN OF SAND OR SHINGLE SETTLEMENT AROUND A WRECK

DIRECTION OF DOMINANT CURRENTS/TIDAL FLOW

Sand or shingle is shifted from the side or end of the wreck facing the flow and builds up as a bank upon the opposite quarter. A scour forms where the sand has been removed. Where the bank will be depends on how the wreck came to rest.

hunt more actively for further food.

Under tragic circumstances, the *Bretagne* had been lost, but as a result there arose a veritable oasis for the new life that came to clothe both her hull and her secret heart. So, in a way, it seemed almost fitting when men and women returned to the wreck, to draw their own harvest from the wealth that now swam or swarmed upon her decks. People to whose ranks we both belong. Anglers.

Charter-skippers, exploring the wreck for the first time, soon realized its potential. They were quick to form parties which saw anglers making some very large catches of fish, but which also resulted in a further hazard to both divers and the inhabitants of the wreck,

namely the tackle which was broken off and sometimes trailed yards of line which could wrap around or trap the unwary. Other skippers, hearing of their peers' successes, formed their own parties to line up and have a crack at the huge numbers of fish.

Inevitably, these stocks were soon reduced, but every season tells its own story and it is still possible to make good catches of a wide variety of species, given the right conditions, tackle and bait. The *Bretagne* may be suffering from a temporary shortage of guests, but she foundered in a seasonal resort and constantly advertises for new residents with the abundance of food which surrounds her.

Over the seasons, many strange and

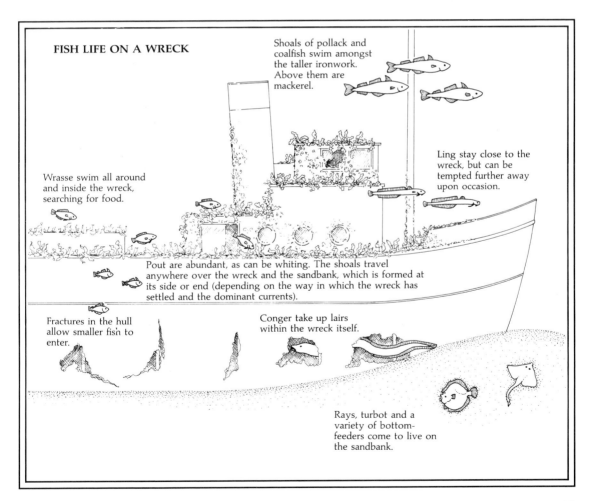

FISH LIFE ON A WRECK

Shoals of pollack and coalfish swim amongst the taller ironwork. Above them are mackerel.

Ling stay close to the wreck, but can be tempted further away upon occasion.

Wrasse swim all around and inside the wreck, searching for food.

Pout are abundant, as can be whiting. The shoals travel anywhere over the wreck and the sandbank, which is formed at its side or end (depending on the way in which the wreck has settled and the dominant currents).

Fractures in the hull allow smaller fish to enter.

Conger take up lairs within the wreck itself.

Rays, turbot and a variety of bottom-feeders come to live on the sandbank.

unusual guests will undoubtedly come to answer this advertisement in their own, inimitable fashion. The angler, when he or she comes to call, can do much worse than to become familiar with the qualities and the attributes of the many inhabitants of the wreck. Some of the species will already be familiar to many, if not most, anglers, but the difference between the successful wreck-angler and the 'chuck it and chance it brigade' almost invariably lies in their depth of knowledge and the rationale employed within each of their tackles.

In this book, I intend to show that there is far more to wreck fishing than simply dropping a predictable tackle over the side of the boat for a handful of well-documented species. There are far more fish to be found than many people might think, and to realize this potential, it is best to start by thinking about the way in which different species have adapted to the conditions found upon the majority of British wrecks: the low level of light, the shelter that the wreck provides, the currents and the unique proliferation of food.

Take, for example, the question of light. Little penetrates to the majority of wrecks, situated as they are in substantial depths of water, so the fish which are found there have become adapted to make the most efficient use of such light as there is at their disposal. One means of doing this is to extend the range of their vision. Consequently, instead of being restricted to the limited forward vision that human beings employ, most species of fish have developed swivel-action, slightly protuberant eyes that enable them to see through nearly 360 degrees. However, despite this increased efficiency, the deeper a fish goes, the less light penetrates and the less it can depend upon sight alone. In order to compensate for this, fish have developed both bodily characteristics and a unique 'sixth sense' that enables them to navigate in perfect safety in conditions where we, unaided, simply couldn't function.

An example of such a bodily characteristic is found in such species as ling, where a barbule can be seen projecting from the lower jaw. Pout also have barbules, and so do many of the species found in deeper water. Essentially, these barbules are studded with taste cells, which allow the fish to identify potential food as it hunts or roots through marine vegetation. It may not have seen something that was hiding, but its touch and taste may invite a second, closer look. Now we can only speculate about the type of information which fish get from such extremities, but isn't it reasonable to assume that it enables the fish to distinguish quite clearly between living tissue and dead? And if this is the case, then how might fish react to bait which has been taken from a fish which was not only dead but may also have been frozen and therefore is still at an unnaturally low temperature? A small point, perhaps, but examine for yourself the difference in your catches when you use fresh bait and frozen. As an alternative, if you cannot get hold of fresh bait, cut any strips while the bait is still frozen, and then pop them into a bucket of water and give them plenty of time to thaw out before you reach your destination.

I have already mentioned a 'sixth sense', by which I refer to a fish's ability to detect deviations in the rebounded vibrations caused by its own swimming motion through the water; information which is extracted through the nerve endings studded along its lateral line. This extra sense allows the fish not only to manoeuvre between rocks and obstructions in the dark, but also to detect the vibrations from the movements of other fish which might be travelling in its immediate vicinity. Consequently, both hunter and hunted, depending upon their sensitivity to such vibrations, can make use of them either to evade or to precipitate capture.

Apart from this very useful sensory device, some species have developed other features which enable them either to hunt more effectively or to evade capture altogether. Some simply swim as close as they can to rocks or the hull of a wreck, almost hugging the surface so that the background echo from the surroundings masks their presence and confuses the 'sixth sense' of any predators in the vicinity. While the hunter tries to pinpoint its position, the smaller fish has usually made good its escape. On the other hand, in an attempt to counter this, and also the effective use of camouflage, some predators, such as shark, have evolved the ability to detect the weak electrical emissions from a living organism, enabling them to strike with both certainty and pinpoint accuracy.

In this armoury of evolution, where the struggle never ends and the only goal is survival, it is not surprising that fish have also developed a highly sophisticated and accurate sense of smell. Take, for example, the humble dogfish, which is often the first to the angler's bait. Its wide-spaced nostrils are well equipped to detect and follow up on even the faintest scents. However, from an angler's point of view, this must surely mean that the stronger-smelling the bait, the greater the chances of drawing a fish to it. Also, if fish are alert to nuances of smell, which is a reasonable assumption, then surely our bait should not be tainted by decomposition — unless we are fishing for scavenging species — but should be as fresh and inviting as possible. This is nowhere more true than when wreck fishing. After all, your bait is competing with all the first-class appetizers that draw fish to the wreck in the first place.

To try and see this more clearly, let us suppose that a restaurant, on its opening day, filled its windows and its tables with a superb range of meals and then invited the public in to sample at will. You come in for a bite to eat and find a mouldy cheese sandwich on the floor. Would you eat the sandwich, or would you look instead at the wide range of tempting delicacies on display? Substitute stale bait for the sandwich and you can see why I think that fresh bait and superb presentation, which I will cover in some detail in Chapter 3, are so vitally important to building up good catches on the wrecks.

Looking at the alternatives which fish have available, it seems hard to understand why they should ever take an angler's bait. I think one of the main reasons why they do is the fact that anglers' offerings are easy to find, need very little energy to scoop up and should, quite frankly, be only a little less fresh than the food the fish are feeding on in the first place. After all, going back to the restaurant analogy, even *you* might let yourself be tempted by an appetizing morsel, left out in full view for extended periods of time, if the main course was trying desperately to hide or run away.

So far, I have dealt with the capabilities of fish and their adaptation to their environment. However, before closing this chapter, there are two further points which I want to raise in some detail. The first of these is the effects upon fish of changing levels of pressure. It is unfortunate, but in wreck-fishing you must be prepared for very few species to survive the pressure changes as you haul them from the depths to the surface. Wrasse, conger and dogfish can all be safely returned, but species such as pollack and ling will almost invariably have to be humanely killed.

Putting the matter very simply, inside most species of bony fish there is an organ — called a swim-bladder — which either inflates (with a mixture of nitrogen and oxygen secreted from the blood) or deflates, according to whether the fish is descending or rising in the water. In both cases, these actions alter the specific gravity of the fish, thus helping it to maintain its position at a particular depth. Now the processes of inflation and deflation are normally accomplished over an extended period of time: the change of pressure occurs little by little rather than suddenly and dramatically (although species such as hake, which have a very muscular swim-bladder, can accomplish much quicker changes of depth than say whiting or cod).

Let us suppose that you hook a large cod, bringing it fairly quickly to the surface. As it is pulled through the water, it is subjected to the sudden changes of pressure that it naturally avoids. The swim-bladder, which is nowhere near as muscular as that of the hake, has no chance to compensate for the demands being made upon it and will often erupt through the fish's intestines and lodge in its mouth. The only humane thing to do then is to kill it as soon as you get it aboard.

The second and last point that I wish to make is that the serious wreck-angler must always bear in mind the state of the tides. Every wreck will be subject to its own unique set of local conditions, but you will find that many are virtually unfishable on the stronger spring tides. Some people might decide to soldier on with wire line and several pounds of lead, but it is not a pleasant way to fish, nor does it make for an enjoyable day. Frankly, it can become both tedious and exhausting. The best thing to do, before you book any trip, anywhere, is to get in contact with an experienced skipper, tell him what dates you have available and ask him which he thinks would prove to be the most productive. He should, if he knows his business, give you good advice so that you can invest both your money and your time profitably. However, there is no compulsion to book there and then. If you feel unhappy with the advice being offered, then simply thank the skipper, ring off and try a few others.

A couple of calls later and you might decide to go back to the first skipper, or you might like the sound of another. Either way, you will usually find that the result is well worth the price of a few minutes on the telephone. It is, after all, a buyer's market with skippers competing for your money. You want to get the best value that you possibly can and they, or at least the decent ones, want you to make the best catches that you possibly can. That way you will be happy and want to come back to fish with them again. They get repeat business. You get good fishing. Both sides come out happy.

At least, that's the theory . . .

CHAPTER ONE

CHOOSING THE RIGHT TACKLE

There is a variety of outfits that can be usefully employed in British wreck fishing, some quite light, some extremely heavy. There is, however, no one outfit which can be used exclusively for every species of fish. Their sheer diversity of size dictates that at least two different outfits, perhaps more, will be necessary if you are going to get the best possible sport from the wrecks that you visit. After all, it is pointless going for conger – which can grow to well over 100 lb (45 kg) in weight – with the same rod that you would use for a 3–10 lb (1·4–4 kg) red bream. Similarly, a 30 lb (13·6 kg) coalfish needs quite different tackle from either of the aforementioned.

If you are going to get maximum enjoyment, then you will find it helpful to have more than one set of tackle at your disposal. However, the wreck angler has a very tangible asset in the form of the skipper, who will almost invariably have a wide range of tackle on board the boat and available for hire. Anyone just starting can pay for a day's use of equipment, and thus get a taste of the sport and see if he or she wants to take it further. Unfortunately, there is as wide a diversity in the quality of tackle available for hire as there is in choice of skippers. Some boats offer excellent tackle, with tackle companies, like Shimano, setting them up with the very best of their range. These are advertised in the tackle brochures of manufacturers and offer the distinct advantage of allowing you to try before you buy. On the other hand there are boats offering tackle that has been bought for

no other reason than it is cheap to replace. The best thing to do, if you have no tackle of your own, is to approach the secretary of your local angling club and see which boats they regularly use. Very often you will find that the club has built up good relationships with a number of skippers in different parts of the country. It is quite likely that the secretary will already have a nodding acquaintance with the type of tackle which they keep on board and will be able to point you in the right direction.

Once past the initial stages, when you have decided that you are definitely going to invest in some tackle, then take your time, shop around and be prepared to put a lot of money into the gear that you choose. Unlike shore-fishing, where the performance of moderate outfits is often disguised by the relatively small number of large fish which come along, wreck fishing offers no such disguise to poor-quality tackle. You can – and will – encounter some very large fish. Your tackle has to be man enough for the job and, quite frankly, you will soon discover that quality does not come cheaply. Reels will almost always be the most expensive item to buy, varying in price from £75 to several hundred, but, fortunately, some very good rods are available at relatively modest prices, say from £30 to £100. The prices that you pay will also vary widely with the type of outfit which you want. A good conger or sharking outfit might cost in the region of £400. Alternatively, a pollack outfit might set you back only a quarter of that price.

There are, of course, cheaper outfits available. At the bottom end of the market there are solid fibreglass rods which can sell for as little as £13. After that there are a number of hollow glass rods, ranging from reasonably good to absolutely awful, then carbon-fibre composites, pure carbon rods and then carbon mixtures with high-tech materials such as boron or silicon carbide. Generally, you will find that the more expensive rods have more power, are lighter to hold, have rings which are much more resistant to corrosion and/or roller tips, or rollers throughout, and will give you far greater control and confidence upon hooking a larger fish. It is a similar story with reels, some of which can be purchased for as little as £50. They can, of course, catch fish, but they have limitations which soon show up if you start going regularly rather than once or twice a year. Most of the time, the problem is the drag, but you could also find spools buckling under pressure, side plates distorting and other problems which, while not stopping the reel from winding in, can totally spoil the feel of it.

The main problem — with all tackle for

A Shakespeare Fulmar, one of the cheapest lever drags available. Regular servicing is a must if you are going to get the best from such a reel.

wreck-fishing — is usually that anglers have unrealistic expectations of the capabilities of their tackle. As I have said before, there is no one, all-purpose, wreck outfit but there are many anglers who try to make their tackle do this particular job. The result is that reels designed for medium-weight fish fail when pitted against heavy-weights; similarly rods which might do for inshore boat-fishing simply fold under the pressure from some of the bigger fish that live on the wrecks. On the other hand, those same outfits might do very well for legering with tackle and baits designed for some of the smaller species that you find on wrecks — species such as wrasse, spur-dogs, flatfish and bass. It is a question of fitting the right tool to the job and that, quite frankly, is where a number of anglers fail.

To help you choose the most appropriate tackle, I have drawn up a table (opposite) which lists particular class outfits — these classes being linked to line strength in the ratings suggested by the International Game Fishing Association (IGFA) — against species or methods which you might like to try. You will find that more than one outfit may be recommended for a particular species, graded according to the size of the individual fish that you might normally expect to catch. This should be helpful, but please bear in mind that the list is not intended to be comprehensive. It is a question of different anglers feeling comfortable with different tackle. Some anglers fish for pollack with much lighter gear than I would use, even though I have fished for them with a light multiplier matched to an uptide boatcaster. To include every outfit with which it is possible to catch pollack would simply serve to make the chart too general to be of use. Therefore, I have listed practical outfits which can be comfortably used to catch the particular species in question. Which you choose is up to you. You may decide that a 30 lb (13·6 kg) outfit can be used for so many different types of wreck-fishing that it is best simply to go for this, plus a 50 lb (22·7 kg) outfit for conger. Alternatively, you might like

Class of Outfit	Species or Method
20 lb (9·1 kg)	Light legering for wrasse etc.
	Drifting for small to medium pollack
	Feathering for bait
	Bream and small predators
30 lb (13·6 kg)	Light to medium legering
	Drifting for pollack and coalfish
	Ling, turbot, rays, angler-fish
	Feathering for bait
	Single pirk and lure-fishing
50 lb (22·7 kg)	Pirk and multi-rigs
	Conger
	Blue shark
80 lb (36·3 kg)	Conger and shark, all British species
Uptide boatcaster/ medium multiplier	Same as for 20 lb class

the sport available with uptide boatcasters and decide to go for one of these, a 30 lb (13·6 kg) outfit for larger pollack and ling, when they are in evidence, and an 80 lb (36·3 kg) class rod for conger and shark.

RODS
In this section I am going to list briefly some points to watch out for when you come to buy a rod. I am also going to mention some of the rods which are available at the time of writing and which either I or some of my friends have tested. Ten of the things you ought to bear in mind are:

1 *Rings*   These should be of reasonable quality and quantity, distances between them decreasing in sensible ratio from butt to tip. If you

sight down the rod you should immediately discern a tunnel-like effect with each ring appearing to be neatly framed by its successor. They should all be in alignment and, if the rod is 50 lb (22·7 kg) class or over, the tip ring should be of the roller variety. If you are intending to use wire line, then all the rings will need to be rollers.

2 *Grips*   Wrecking is not usually a 'put the rod down and watch the tip' job. You are going to be holding the rod for most of the day so you need to make sure that the grips are both comfortable and securely attached, especially making sure that they will not twist or slide under pressure.

3 *Spigots*   These are also known as joints. These are put under a lot of pressure and need to be adequately reinforced, especially on the female section.

4 *Whippings*   These should be of good quality and properly sealed − not prone to cracking under pressure due to the finish having been incorrectly accelerated by the use of excessive hardener.

5 *The blank*   This should be powerful with a sensitive tip for the detection of bites. Lightness makes for comfort, but this should not be achieved at the expense of strength.

6 *The reel seat*   This should be secure and of good quality, resistant to corrosion and engineered to avoid any distortion which might allow the reel to move or twist.

7 *Appearance*   Everyone likes a rod to look nice, but be wary of flashy trimmings which might disguise shoddy workmanship. What you need is a professional appearance with attention to detail. Far better to be plain and effective than gawdy and trash.

8 *Matching of materials*   All materials used in the construction of the rod should be properly matched; for example, a lightweight blank should not be encumbered with an old-fashioned heavy handle.

9 *Rod quality*   Get the assistant to hold the tip of the rod and put some pressure on it −

steady and sustained, not sudden. If the rod creaks, feels dodgy or fails to recover immediately then reject it.

10 *Value for money* Be confident in your own mind that you are getting your money's worth. Some mail-order companies will offer rods at very good discounts, but they are more difficult to deal with in the event of problems. You either buy locally, preferably from a shop with a reputation for excellent service, or you shop through the mail-order advertisements in the magazines and try and save yourself some pennies or, as sometimes happens, a considerable number of pounds.

As you can imagine, there are many rods which answer the above criteria beautifully. However, it is not my intention to create a tackle brochure and I have therefore restricted the rods in the following list to a few which I have tested and which did very well. There are even a couple of lower-priced rods amongst them!

DAM Megalite Uptide CR, 2341 031 Megalite IGFA (30 lb/13·6 kg class), 2341 051 and 081 Megalite IGFA CR (50 and 80 lb/22·7 and 36·3 kg class).

Daiwa GCB 20, 30 and 50R Seahunter in classes 20, 30 and 50 lb (9·1, 13·6 and 22·7 kg).

Ryobi WR65 50 lb (22·7 kg) Wreck-King.

Shimano Twin-power boat-rods in all classes. Twin-power uptider in heavier casting size (4–10 oz/113–850 g).

REELS

Take a trip out from nearly any port which you care to mention and you will find that almost every angler on board is using a multiplier, a reel which derives its name from the arrangement of its gears. These are designed in such a manner that the spool revolves several times for every turn of the handle, making the reels very smooth and efficient for the retrieval of line. The speed of the retrieve will, however, depend upon how much line you put on the spool. When the spool is empty, its diameter is comparatively small. A full turn of the handle may, for argument's sake, wind on only a few inches of line. As the spool fills, that diameter is augmented by the line itself, increasing the amount of line which is recovered so that, by the time the spool is nearly full, the amount of line being recovered with every turn of the handle is several times the original few inches. It therefore makes sense to keep the spool as full as possible so that you get the fastest possible retrieve.

There are many different models of multipliers available, but they are usually fitted with either star- or lever-drag systems, these being designed so that a fish can pull line from the reel against a pressure that has been predetermined by the angler. The difference between them is that a star drag is adjusted by means of a star-shaped nut set just below the handle while the lever drag is adjusted, as its name suggests, by a lever set at the side of the reel. When the lever drag is at its bottom setting, the spool is completely free-running for the release of line. By pushing the lever forward, the angler can increase the amount of pressure until he feels that it has reached the

The Ryobi SLE 320, a star-drag multiplier that has been designed for use with light to medium outfits.

right degree of resistance. If he wants to increase the pressure to the point of almost locking the spool, then the chances are that he will have to push down a special button in order to reach it. This is a safety feature which has been designed to prevent line breakages caused by putting too much pressure on a struggling fish too early in the fight. All in all, this simple but effective system makes lever drags much easier, quicker and far less fiddly to adjust than star drags, although the latter are still very efficient and can be pre-set with a precision difficult to match with lever drags. You might, for example, set the drag on a multiplier so that it allows the release of line just before its breaking point is reached. With a star drag, which is independent of the spool-release system, this setting will remain at that point until you decide to alter it. If you want to lower your weight to the seabed, you simply disengage the clutch by a simple on/off mechanism and the spool releases line freely and quickly. When you reach the bottom you re-engage the clutch, and with it the pre-set star drag, by simply moving a lever or just turning the handle. With a lever drag, which you have to slacken right off to get your gear

to the fish in the first place, you will have to re-set to this point each time that you drop your tackle in the water. On the other hand, if you suddenly find that you need to put more pressure on whatever fish you are playing, you can do this more easily and quickly with a lever drag than a star drag. Which you use is up to you, but, at the time of writing, star drags are probably far more commonly used than lever drags. Both are perfectly good systems and available in a range of sizes that will cope with every wreck-fishing contingency.

Another feature possessed by some, but not all, multipliers is known as a level-wind. This is essentially a line guide which travels along a worm drive and ensures even distribution of line. It is incredibly handy when struggling against a larger fish, enabling you to lock your grip around the rod and forget about trying to guide the line on the spool with your thumb. Level-winds simplify line retrieval considerably although some anglers don't like them for exactly that reason, almost as if it was cheating! Personally, I much prefer a multiplier with a level-wind to one without but I suggest that you try both before you make up your own mind.

The Ryobi Trymaster 70CL, an excellent reel — at a very reasonable price — for use with uptide boatcasters.

A star-drag multiplier, in this instance the dependable Ryobi SLE 340 — very useful for larger species.

If using a level-wind troubles some people, then you should hear the comments made about using such multipliers as the Ryobi AD101SS, an electric reel that is both incredibly efficient and extremely rugged! Now whether you agree with the notion of a powered reel or shudder at the thought, Ryobi have taken the concept and produced a reel which, although expensive, is ideally suited to heavier wreck fishing. The power facility takes the boredom out of simply bringing up your hook to check the bait, but can be ignored if you want to play any fish that you catch manually. It is a reel which is well worth having a look at, and I mention it in greater detail in Chapter 7.

Whatever reel you decide to get, you must make sure that it is strong enough to contend with the severe strain that wreck fishing will impose upon it. It is no use taking a light carbon boat-reel and putting it under such stress that the side plates distort, the gears suffer and the drag is totally unable to cope. This is a problem particularly pertinent to multipliers fitted with a level-wind. You may find, for example, that most level-winds fall within the light to medium categories, with a

The Ryobi AD101SS Electric reel, perhaps the forerunner of a whole generation of powered reels.

limited choice available for heavier work. Daiwa, for example, produce a range of level-winds for light to medium work – the Super Doutsuki series – but their heavier multipliers – the larger Sealines – all depend on the angler manually guiding the line onto the reel with his or her thumb. They are, however, sturdily constructed reels which will stand up to an awful lot of nonsense. They are also fitted with lugs to which a shoulder harness can be attached. This is a nice touch which I would like to see on a few more reels, especially because of the invaluable assistance which it affords to anglers suffering from a range of disabilities.

Shimano Beastmasters have similar provision for the attachment of a shoulder harness, but are otherwise quite different in appearance from the dependable Sealines. These two-speed lever drags are superbly engineered and designed to take anything that you can throw at them. They are, quite frankly, in a class of their own but with the inevitable disadvantage of carrying a price tag that reflects this attention to detail and quality. Don't get me wrong! I firmly believe that these reels represent excellent value for money, but with a starting price in excess of £230 there are many anglers who would have difficulty affording this amount. Those who can will find themselves with a superb reel which is unlikely to let them down. For those who can't, there are still a number of reels on the market which will perform in a respectable manner. Frankly, I could write a book that looks at nothing but the pros and cons of the wide range of multipliers available on the market today. Instead I have drawn up a short table (opposite) recommending a few good multipliers for the categories of outfits. Every one mentioned has been tested either by me or by a small, select circle of friends, each of whom is an angler of considerable experience. It is not intended to be comprehensive, but should offer a range of no-nonsense reels to suit different tastes and different budgets.

Looking at the table I am aware that there is

Class of Outfit	Suggested Reels
Light to medium work (Includes uptide boatcasters, 20 and 30 lb/9·1 and 13·6 kg classes)	Shimano Triton lever drag Daiwa GS60 Super Doutsuki Daiwa GS70 Super Doutsuki Daiwa GS50 Super Doutsuki Ryobi SLE 320 Ryobi SLE 330 Shimano TBMG Beastmaster (12/30)
50 lb (22·7 kg) class	Ryobi SLE 340 Ryobi AD101SS Electric Daiwa SL 400H Daiwa SL 450H Daiwa SL 600H Shimano TBMG Beastmaster (20/50) Shimano TBM Beastmaster (TBM 4/0, 30/50, 50/80)
80 lb (36·3 kg) class	Ryobi AD101SS Electric Shimano TBM Beastmasters (50/80, 80/130) Daiwa SL 900H Daiwa SL 910

lighter rod and reel than an angler who fishes wrecks 400–500 ft (120–150 m) deep with a tide race that demands several pounds of lead to get the bait or lure to the fish. To a large extent, your choice of reel will be determined by the conditions found in your immediate locality, simply because the chances are that you will make many more trips from your home port than 'away' trips. Having said that, at least one of the models listed should do you really well for both, but I do suggest that you have a good chat with an angler who regularly fishes in the area. His advice will be invaluable in helping you to select the model that most exactly fits your requirements and balances the rod which you have chosen.

LINES

Three main types of line are available to wreck-anglers, namely nylon monofilament, wire line and Dacron (which can be difficult to get hold of in the heavier breaking strains). All of them have their advantages and their disadvantages. Nylon monofilament, for example, is the cheapest and most commonly used, but can be adversely affected — albeit over a period of time — by sunlight. It also has a greater diameter than wire and tends to stretch under pressure, which neither of the others do. On the plus side, it is relatively cheap and is far easier to tie than either of the other materials.

If you are fishing in a strong tide, however, then wire line has the distinct advantage that its significantly lower diameter offers far less for the tide to get hold of; this gives you the very practical benefit of being able to reduce vastly the amount of lead needed to hold bottom. It has absolutely no stretch and puts you immediately in touch with any fish that takes the bait, often enabling you to get a fish away from cover far more quickly and more easily than if you were using nylon line. Frankly, if the wrecks that you fish have a strong tide race, then the advantages of wire outweigh the disadvantages of its expense and difficulty to tie. Generally, it is often a good

a vast difference in the capacities of some of the reels, even though they may be listed against the same class of outfit. However, as a range of reels, there is a model to cater for nearly every eventuality which you are ever likely to face. If you live in a part of the country where the deepest wreck lies in some 200 ft (60 m) of water and the tide race is only moderate, then you can get away with a much idea to have two spools for your reel: one loaded with nylon for general use, the other with wire for when the tide starts to race.

It is inadvisable to use Dacron as this has a high absorption rate; as the diameter of the line swells, so it offers a greater surface to the tide than either nylon or wire. To counter this you would have to increase the amount of lead significantly.

Whatever line you decide upon, expense is a point which is well worth bearing in mind. With lines, as with anything else, you get what you pay for. There is little point in paying hundreds of pounds for a decent outfit and then putting on thick, inefficient nylon because it is cheap and you get lots on a spool. If you are going to buy nylon then you want a low-stretch line that is supple and offers a high knot-strength. The chances are that a 1000 metre spool of quality line will set you back quite a lot, say about £40, depending on the line strength that you want, but it is an investment worth making when you consider the strain that a decent fish will put upon it. You should also be wary when you come to examine the current spate of low-diameter 'thin' nylon lines. These can be very brittle, often as a result of the line having started life with a normal diameter and then being stretched to make it thinner. Personally, I use Siglon Marine, which is a normal-diameter line, for general wreck fishing and keep a reel loaded with Tide-Cheater wire line for when the tide is a bit strong. Neither are particularly cheap, but they are effective.

Another line which I ought to mention is nylon-covered wire. This is available in short lengths — say 25 metre spools — and is ideal for making traces for conger. It can be tied using crimps or the bimini hitch; the latter is very much stronger and is explained in detail in Chapter 4.

WEIGHTS

If you are going to do a serious amount of wreck fishing then it is a good idea to buy a couple of moulds and start making your own weights, which is a much cheaper way of doing things. Getting hold of lead is not a problem as it can be obtained through a variety of sources and is fairly inexpensive. For example, I often get mine free from tyre-balancing stations, which are sometimes only too glad to get rid of the old weights which they have taken off their customers' cars. If you ask, when you are having a new tyre fitted, you will often find the staff particularly helpful! The only other raw material necessary is some thin-gauge stainless-steel wire for the eyes. This can be purchased through most tackle shops and occasionally from builders' merchants.

Equipment is simple. You will need a vice, clamp or similar for keeping the mould tightly shut during casting, an old saucepan, an old metal tin and a spoon for skimming the rubbish from the top of the molten lead. The ring of a cooker is perfectly adequate for a source of heat but you must ensure that the room is well ventilated. Lead is a cumulative poison and can build up in your system. Obviously you don't want that, either for yourself or your family, so please take all necessary precautions.

Before making your weights, there are a few points which will help you to make them safely and well. A good tip, for example, is to pre-heat the mould so that the lead takes slightly longer to cool. This will not only result in a better appearance, but will also have the advantage of drying the mould thoroughly before you start casting. This is important as any moisture that remains will be trapped and driven out as steam when you pour in the first lot of lead. That can be quite dangerous.

When it comes to buying a mould, you will find that your choice is limited to the few boat moulds available. Personally, I like the bell weight from Ajusti and the Bopedo from DCA. I use the former for general leger and the latter for working rubber lures off the bottom. You might also find it helpful to get a couple of moulds that will enable you to cast a selection of smaller weights from 3–8 oz (85–227 g). These will be helpful for feathering for mackerel and when using lighter tackle for breaming, light leger etc.

SWIVELS, SPLIT LINKS AND RUNNING BOOMS

There is a variety of swivels available on the market, but for general work you need only bother with the very strong and corrosion-resistant Berkley swivels. These are small for their strength, making your tackle neat and streamlined, and very efficient. Get a range of these in various sizes and match them with 'easy links' for quick changing of tackles. ('Easy links' are stainless wire links which are designed for swift attachment or removal. They are strong, resistant to corrosion and relatively inexpensive.)

Besides some easy links, you will find it helpful to get in stock a range of split rings in good-quality wire and larger sizes. These will be invaluable for pirk tackles.

Running booms enable the weight to slide freely on the line. This may arguably give any fish that takes your bait a short space of time before it realizes that there is resistance and spits out the bait. There are a few patterns on the market, but I usually stick to Ajusti sliders, zip sliders or even just a swivel with the line running through one eye and a split link to the weight on the other. Almost all of these booms are improved when you match them with some stiff plastic tubing and a couple of beads. These can be helpful in presenting the trace away from the weight so that the tackle streams out with the current and doesn't tangle.

LURES AND PIRKS

Lures are artificial baits which are designed to make a fish attack them in the mistaken belief that they are edible. So are pirks, which are made out of metal tubing filled with lead and weigh from a few ounces to a couple of pounds (60 gm to 1 kg). Basically, lures for

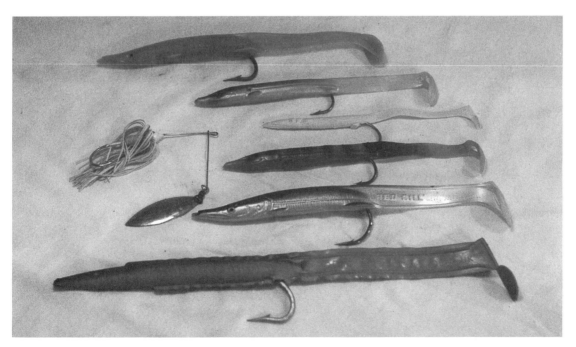

A selection of Redgills, Eddystone Eels and a Roland Martin spinner. All are effective for catching pollack.

wreck fishing comprise: soft latex lures for pollack and coalfish, ranging from American imports to the excellent and popular Redgills, Eddystone and Delta Eels; spinners such as the Roland Martin bladed spoons; and plugs, such as the Rapala Originals, Slivers, rattle 'n' raps and the magnums. Muppets, which are essentially latex squid, are good for cod and ling, with white, yellow and orange arguably the best colours.

Generally, in deep water, colour seems to be more important with regard to soft-bodied lures than it is plugs. I carried out a statistical investigation on the effectiveness of different rubber eels during the second year of my degree and found that red, black, red-and-black combinations and fluorescent-orange eels all seemed to work better than other colours for catching pollack. Similarly I found that there was a definite correlation between the size of fish caught and the size of lure used. When I analysed the results of over 3,000 separate drops, the message was unmistakable:

the size of fish caught increased as the size of lure increased. So, if you want to catch bigger fish, I suggest that you go for the biggest lures that you can get! Pirks can be either bought or home-made, but they work best when the treble hook on the lower ring is adorned with either a muppet or a squid. If you want to make them yourself, all you have to do is get hold of some good-quality chrome tubing, fill it with lead, then cut it into different lengths to give you different weights of pirk. Make sure that you don't cut it straight across; rather turn the hacksaw so that it cuts across the tube at an angle of approximately 45 degrees. File or grind the ends smooth, then drill through the raised sections at either end so that you can thread on a split ring and swivel at the top and a split ring, treble hook and muppet at the bottom.

An alternative method of manufacture is to squeeze a piece of tubing shut, drill the flattened section for attachment of a split ring, then fill the rest of the tube with the desired

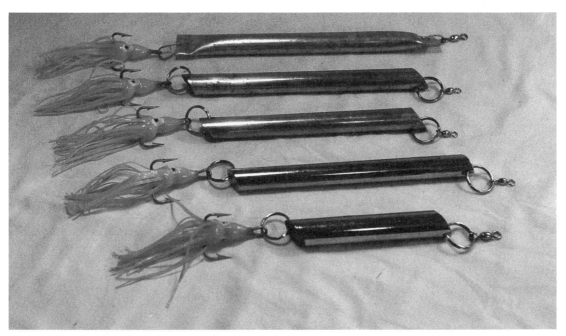

A selection of shop-bought and home-made pirks.

amount of lead. Cut the tube above the lead, then flatten this and drill to accept the second split ring. I have caught fish on these but not as many as I have caught on pirks made the first way.

BUTT PADS

As their name suggests, butt pads are a support for the butt of the rod. They are worn around the angler's waist and are designed to protect the pit of the stomach/top of the groin from becoming sore as a result of continuous pumping of the rod, an action which can be painful because, without a butt pad, you need to brace the rod against your body. Pumping drives the butt firmly home and you can get very sore if you have no protection. I personally feel butt pads are essential equipment. If you ever get a day when the pollack really come on the feed, then you will be grateful, at the end of the day, that you spent £10 or so which a butt pad costs.

HOOKS

Hooks are not mentioned in any great detail here, because the sizes and types that I use will be described in the chapters on each species.

Butt pads make very good sense, especially as a hard day's fishing can be extremely uncomfortable.

You would probably be advised to ensure that you have reasonable numbers of O'Shaughnessies and Vikings in sizes 2 (for general bottom-feeders) through to 8/0 (for conger). The points of the hooks should be short, sharp and strong. A long point breaks or blunts easily. Bronzed hooks are best avoided as they tend to corrode very quickly. Stainless steel is best, but it is also a good idea to have some very strong Aberdeens in sizes 4 and 2 (for smaller bottom-feeders) and in sizes 4/0 and 6/0 (for turbot and rays).

CLOTHING

Warm clothing is essential for wrecking. When you get out of sight of land you can find yourself getting colder by the minute, and bitterly so on occasions. If you are going out in the winter you would be well advised to buy yourself a thermal inner suit and a suitably waterproof, windproof thermal outer. There are several available on the market but, once again, they do not come cheaply. You can easily spend £150 on cold-weather gear, but it is an essential investment if you are going to get any kind of enjoyment out of wrecking throughout a cold winter's day. Make sure that any thermal outer suit has a hood. This can be very useful, particularly if you get yourself a padded hat of the deerstalker variety. This protects your ears from the cold while the hood pulls tight against the rim of the hat and seals in the heat.

Protecting your extremities is very important. Footwear should be waterproof and warm, but also able to be kicked off quickly if you have the misfortune to fall in the water. Wellingtons fill and act like twin weights, pulling you quickly to the bottom. They should be avoided. You also need to keep your hands warm. Thermal mittens are more useful than gloves because you can pull the covering back from your fingers, tie any knots that you have to, then simply put the cover back where it belongs.

ACCESSORIES

There are all sorts of things that you can buy — and justify if you want to — but here is a brief list of some things that may prove useful when you get aboard:

1 *Nail Clippers* Better than scissors for cutting strong line.

2 *Pliers* Useful for wire line and traces, also for any emergency repairs that you might have to do on equipment.

3 *Filleting knife* A good quality blade for preparing bait and gutting the catch.

4 *A spool of monofilament* For filling your reel in case you lose a lot of line on the wreck.

5 *A spool of heavy monofilament* For traces and a spool of nylon-covered wire for the same reason.

6 *Hook sharpener.*

7 *Sea-sickness tablets.*

CHAPTER TWO

GETTING AFLOAT

The first time I went out of sight of land on a relatively small boat I was, I must admit, a trifle nervous. That was a feeling that disappeared on the very first drop of my tackle. As I watched it disappear into the depths, my imagination pictured its passage through vast shoals of pollack, being sniffed at by a passing shark, then being seized by a coalfish of such stamina and power that it would take the better part of an hour to boat it.

So much for imagination. I caught nothing on that drop, or the next, or indeed the drop after that. Instead I watched intently as fish after fish hit my companions' lures, then finally surfaced with one last swirl as we swore in frustration. Prime, beautiful cod, each one weighing between 15 and 28 lb (6·8 and 12·7 kg) — in the middle of a cod ban! Each one of those fish had to be returned, our spirits sinking with them as they slipped slowly from sight.

Later, after 3 hours of expectation and disappointment, I finally connected with my first fish from a wreck, a double-figure pollack that hit the lure so hard that it stopped me dead in the retrieve. All at once my hopes, which had been gradually fading, came alive with a surge of excitement, then caught up with the thrill as I played that first fish to the side of the boat. As I watched it come aboard, I marvelled at its sleek perfection, its power, its size . . .

That was the first of three, not large by wrecking standards, but quite enough to arouse and sustain my interest for further trips.

Sustain? Who am I kidding? I couldn't wait to get aboard again. I had to get aboard, to get out from that harbour and catch some more of those big, beautiful fish. My initial trepidation was completely forgotten as I keenly looked forward to my second trip.

That second trip was also the last day I ever listened to the weather forecasters. 'Oh yes', they assured the eager listeners, the very fate of that trip hanging in the balance, 'Oh yes, the wind will drop. It is a force 5 at the moment, but it will drop. By early afternoon, it will have dropped to force 3 and still be on the wane.'

Wonderful! As we steamed out from the harbour, the twin engines propelling the boat at such speed that we seemed almost to skim across the waves, turning the water at our rear so that white horses seemed to prance, to strain to keep up with us, so my mind relived those earlier fights and dreamed of new ones today. It was going to be so special!

Well, I suppose it was. As soon as the skipper called 'Down you go', my tackle streaked over the side and was almost instantly taken by a pollack. Jubilantly I played it aboard, then dropped my tackle down for another, and another! I was thoroughly enjoying myself! Then, all of a sudden, halfway through my fight with another pollack, I suddenly didn't feel terribly well; in fact, as the pollack put up its usual, spirited resistance, I was even tempted to give the rod to someone else to bring it up through the final stages. I didn't, as it happens, but by the time it came aboard I was in no condition to give it any more than a cursory glance; with a feeling of relief, I sank to the deck and lay my head upon the gunwhale, waiting expectantly to be introduced to the joys of a 'technicolour yawn'.

By some mercy, if mercy it was, I was spared that particular ignominy. Instead, I fell asleep where I was, only to be revived by an extremely anxious skipper who thought I had suffered a heart attack and died on the spot! I instantly, if somewhat incoherently, reassured him on this point, trying to convey the impression that my mind was clear even though my body seemed to have temporarily abdicated its functions to another control. I didn't seem to have much luck on this point, so the skipper sympathetically took me below, where another individual was having an even worse time than myself.

Oh, and the weather? Dropped, do I hear you say? Flat calm by early afternoon in total justification of the unerring accuracy of the British weather-forecasting service? Would it surprise you if it wasn't? No? Well, you are right. By the time we turned back for port there were only four out of a dozen anglers who were not somewhere in or between the two stages of sea-sickness. You know what those are, don't you? The first is when you are afraid you are going to die; the second is when you are afraid that you are not. I was well into the first, while my companion was well into the second. Frankly, there were only a few of us who were in any way able to contend with drifting in the teeth of a force 7, rising to force 8, gale. It was not quite what we had expected.

I learned a painful lesson that day. Just because you have no problems with sea-sickness on one boat does not mean to say that you will not have them on another. Always take precautions. It doesn't hurt to be prepared but it certainly takes the fun out of a trip if you are not. Get yourself some sea-sickness tablets — Kwells are good — and take them in strict accordance with the instructions on the packet. If they don't work and you still become ill, well, frankly, the best thing to do is

to get on with it. Nobody wants to hear you suffer. The chances are that they have already been there themselves. Just get on with it quietly.

Personally, on the rare (cough, cough!) occasions that I succumb, I am more annoyed than anything else! There I am, really looking forward to getting hold of some decent fish, and I dare not move from the lavatory in case I redecorate the inside of the skipper's cabin. It is really aggravating! Fortunately, and I mean this seriously, it does not happen that often. The main reason is because I take the necessary precautions. That is a rule which can apply to anybody. So long as you are aware of your limitations you can avoid most of the unpleasantness. For example, I absolutely detest the smell of diesel so, when the skipper starts the engine, I make sure that I am sitting inside the cabin with the door shut, thereby avoiding the great clouds of fumes which can sometimes be given off. Similarly, I don't fish from a position where I am breathing in the exhaust fumes. It is basic common sense, coupled with a motion tablet an hour before we leave the port and my Sea Bands.

Sea Bands are worth a mention as I have seen them work for quite a few people over the years. Basically, the idea is that they prevent motion sickness by exerting a controlled pressure on the Nei-Kuan acupressure point, which is approximately three fingers' width up from the first wrist crease, in the middle of the flexor tendons. Correct positioning is essential for the bands to be effective. However, as no drugs are involved, the bands have the significant advantage of not inducing drowsiness, unlike motion tablets.

Personally, I use both methods. I also take other precautions, not so much additional measures as being careful about what I eat, drink and do in the 24 hours immediately before the trip. For example, if you are feeling tired or unwell before you board then you are that much more vulnerable to sea-sickness. It is therefore essential to get a good nights' sleep before you go. You would also be well advised to eat carefully on both the morning of the trip and the day before. Avoid fatty foods and eating to excess. Don't have a hearty fried breakfast unless you know for certain that you have a cast-iron stomach.

Be doubly careful about what you eat on the actual day. Don't go under the mistaken impression that if you eat nothing there will be nothing to bring up and you will be perfectly all right. It doesn't work that way. Believe me, there is nothing worse than constant dry retching with nothing to bring up. Having an empty stomach doesn't help. It hinders. Take a fairly balanced meal with you: say sandwiches, a couple of apples, a flask of coffee or tea, some rich-tea biscuits and a small bottle of lemonade. Don't take a vacuum flask full of canned soup unless you are a very good traveller. Just be careful what food you choose and eat it sparingly rather than all at once.

Little and often is probably quite a good maxim in this instance.

Whether you suffer from sea-sickness or not, when you go to sea you must be very safety-conscious. The sea can be kind or treacherous, turning from almost flat calm to the most alarming conditions in a very short space of time. If this happens, then you have literally put your life in the hands of the skipper and, for your own peace of mind, you should be confident that he is competent and has all the necessary safety equipment on board the boat. This includes life-jackets for every person, life-rafts, VHF radio, flares, fire-extinguishers, lights, compass, navigation equipment, fog horn. All of these items — and more — should be on board and all should be in perfect working order. From time to time, they will be officially inspected. For your part, you should spend at least a few minutes at the start of

Fast boats, like Striker *out of Torquay, have the speed to get back into port quickly should the need arise.*

each trip ascertaining exactly where everything is and what you should do in the event of an emergency. Don't neglect this. It is very easy to get blasé when going on trip after trip but, quite frankly, if an emergency does occur then you only have the one chance to get out of it safely. It is no use trying to do everything in a blind panic. If the worst happens and the boat comes to grief, then you might find yourself in a very dangerous situation with only seconds to react. Those seconds may be the difference between life and death. They should not be wasted trying to discover where something is.

There is another thing you should bear in mind. It sounds quite silly, but you have to be prepared and able to do it. If the time comes when you have immediately to abandon ship, then you must be able to abandon your tackle and personal possessions without a second thought. They take up room and add weight to the life-rafts and both these factors can jeopardize your safety and the safety of others. Don't waste your chances of survival on a piece of tackle, rod, reel, whatever — no matter how precious it is to you. Just follow the skipper's instructions and be as quick about them as you can. After all, a rod can be replaced, probably with money from the boat's insurance. The same cannot be said about you.

Check that the boat is fully insured and equipped. Then, when you are convinced that everything is in order for the safety of the passengers and crew, turn your attention to the boat itself. This is crucial for determining whether or not any trip will take place. If the boat is fast, then it can get back into port much more quickly than an older, slower vessel. If the weather turns nasty that could be extremely important, both from the viewpoint of safety and for your own personal comfort. The skipper will have the latest weather reports before he sets sail, but, as I have said before, the wind can change direction and do something completely unexpected. If the weather reports sound to be borderline, then it

might be worth going ahead if the boat is fast enough to get you out of trouble quickly. On the other hand, if the boat is slow, only capable of speeds less than 14 knots, then you should consider very seriously whether or not to take the chance. Usually, the skipper will have a pretty good idea, but there are times when his idea of comfortable fishing will be quite at odds with your own. There is little pleasure in fishing when you can only just manage to stand up. Make sure that his idea of what is fishable is the same as your own.

If the weather and everything else is in order, then you can turn your attention to what else the boat has to offer. From an angler's point of view I would consider Decca, or a Decca clone, invaluable. This is a navigation system which makes use of radio signals to pinpoint the exact position of a mark. It is an extremely accurate system and has a variety of features which can help the skipper both to record new, profitable marks and to position the boat accurately over old ones, with the minimum of time being wasted. Every charter-boat should have one, certainly if the intention is to carry predominantly wreck-fishing parties.

An accurate fishfinder or echo-sounder is also very useful. Decca can get you to the mark quickly; the fishfinder can tell you whether there are any fish on it. Obviously, the more accurate it is the better your chances will be of connecting. Some of the cheaper models are serviceable but have so little definition that only 'Jaws' would make an impression! Other models are so accurate that they can detect a single, medium-sized pollack as it swims over a wreck.

So far, I have spoken about what you can expect from the skipper and the boat. There are, however, certain courtesies which you should extend to both the skipper and to the other members of your party, a few simple guidelines which will help to avoid tangles and unpleasantness. The first of these is very simple: namely, be at the appointed place at least 10 minutes early. The skipper will have

Feathering for mackerel — a resource that is cheap and easy to exploit.

Wrasse, often reaching a surprisingly large size, browse through wrecks in shallow water.

The broken hull of a ship offers sanctuary from predators, which it can confuse by masking the movements of smaller fish.

As this underwater photograph by Diana Ingram shows, there is little chance of moving a big conger eel once it has reached the safety of its lair.

The effect upon a vessel of more than half a century underwater, thus providing a haven for many species.

A brace of double-figure pollack, taken from a wreck lying some way off the South Coast.

A blue shark taken off Torquay. Nowadays such fish would be better released to live and fight another day.

An angler-fish waits near the wreck to lure unwary prey to their deaths.

A spotted ray at the side of a wreck. Other rays include thornbacks and blondes.

A specimen pollack with a 6-pounder (2·7 kg) for comparison.

A catch of blonde rays taken aboard Striker of Torquay.

A 64 lb (29 kg) conger taken off Torquay. Fillet of mackerel or smaller fish, such as whiting, make excellent baits for fish of this size.

planned his day carefully, taking into account the tide times, travelling time, strength of currents and tidal races etc., when choosing exactly which mark to fish. If you turn up late then he may not be able to give you as much time on the mark as he had hoped, which can annoy him and be frustrating for the anglers who did turn up on time.

When you get on board, stow your tackle carefully where directed and either stand or sit out of the way. Don't make things awkward for the crew as they prepare to leave the mooring or the harbourside. Get out of their way and leave them to it, unless of course they ask you to do something to help. While you are waiting, you might as well find out the positions of the safety equipment, which are often displayed on a poster. Don't ask a lot of questions straight away; just look for obvious clues then check up with the crew as soon as the boat has left the harbour. By that time, they will be able to answer your questions without being distracted from more immediate duties.

Take a spare rod which has already been set up — minus weight — with mackerel feathers. The skipper will not want the weight on in case it knocks against other rods and causes damage while the boat is in motion. However, you can always put a link on the end of the feathers and a weight in your pocket. That way, you will be able to set up in seconds and start catching mackerel almost right away. Another idea is to take a telescopic rod for catching bait, for example, the DAM California blue 200. Such rods are ideal as not only can they be stored more easily than a full-length rod but they are also sufficiently powerful to double up for light legering for the smaller species. They also have the advantage of being relatively inexpensive.

Take plenty of spare traces and tackle. When you lose your end gear — which you will, from time to time — you can quickly set yourself up again if your tackle is organized and the trace is already tied. That way you will maximize your fishing time. Make sure

that you also have a variety of leads on board, from small ones to big ones, and, if you are legering, use one which is heavy enough to hold bottom. That is a point which you should be aware of all the time. When you feel the lead hit the seabed, put your thumb on the spool and re-engage the clutch so that the spool is no longer free-running. It may appear as if you still ought to give line, but it really is not necessary. You have already reached the bottom and what you are experiencing is the current pushing against the surface of the line. If you give out slack, you will start to create a very large bow between your rod tip and the weight. Eventually this will reach under the boat, depending on which side you are fishing, and cause a lot of tangles and annoyance. Frankly, keeping a tight line may seem a bit strange at first but, once you get used to it, it does save you, and everyone else, a lot of inconvenience.

Lastly, but not least, be considerate towards both the skipper and his boat, which is very often a friend rather than a possession. Chopping up bait or gutting mackerel on the deck instead of on a bait-board may lead to a few choice words if the skipper has already put a board out for you to use. A trip can be ruined by a rotten atmosphere so you might as well do everything you can to keep everyone happy. Listen to what the skipper advises, not just about the boat, but about the fishing itself. He has probably fished whatever wreck you are over on several ocasions and he will know what you are likely to catch, or what methods have proved successful in the past. More than anyone, a good skipper will want you to make a good catch of fish; that way you will be happy, he may have a few fish left on board to sell at the fish market, and his reputation is enhanced rather than jeopardized. There is nothing more annoying to many skippers than watching people fail to catch fish when the fishfinder shows that the wreck is swarming with them and the only reason for failing is because inappropriate methods or bait are being used. This is doubly annoying when the skipper has already told the party what to do and been ignored! Think about it; when you have chartered a boat, you have also chartered both the knowledge and expertise of the skipper. It makes sense to get the best possible benefit from both.

CHAPTER THREE

MAKING THE MOST OF YOUR BAIT

Bait for wreck fishing can be as varied as for fishing from shore. However, over the years, anglers have rejected most of the proliferation of baits available and mackerel, squid and sand-eels have emerged as the baits for wreck-fishing. Unfortunately, this is a reflection of the limited number of species upon which anglers have concentrated rather than a true picture of the effective baits for the variety of fish likely to be encountered on a wreck.

In this chapter, I am going to examine a fairly small number of baits: not just the 'big three', but also prawns, hard-backed crabs — which will take smooth-hound and wrasse — peeler crabs, lugworm and hermit crabs. Between them, these baits make up an effective and versatile list which, although not exhaustive, is nonetheless able to account for almost all species that you are ever likely to meet.

MACKEREL

More than anything else, the mackerel is the mainstay of the wreck-angler's supply of fresh bait. Plentiful, though not occurring in such numbers as formerly, easy to catch and attractive to a variety of species, the mackerel holds the primary advantage that an angler can go to sea with only a set of feathers and, in a short space of time, catch enough mackerel to last him the day. This makes it invaluable to charter-skippers, who see it as the best — and cheapest — means of supplying everyone on board with fresh bait.

Feathers are traditionally used to catch mackerel, these being either three- or six-hook traces which have had feathers whipped to the shanks of the hooks. The angler jigs them up and down in the water, gradually changing the depth until the mackerel shoals are encountered. Then, when a mackerel bites, he simply gives the feathers an additional few seconds — occasionally tempting others to take — before bringing the mackerel on board for unhooking and storage.

Nowadays there is a choice of feathers on the market, ranging from cheaper sets with traditional feathers to more expensive sets like the Hokkai lures, which have a latex body as well as a more sophisticated arrangement of feathers. All of them will catch fish, but you will find that the Hokkais in particular have an appeal which is not limited simply to mackerel. So far I have caught mackerel, scad, pollack, bass, herring, whiting, John Dory and pout upon these lures, so I don't mind paying the bit extra which they cost. They are also useful because they can tempt some of the smaller — and bigger — species from the wreck itself, thus providing an alternative tactic for days when the wreck simply is not producing in the manner which you hoped.

When using traditional feathers, many anglers like to trim them about $\frac{1}{2}$ in (13 mm) from the bend of the hook. The idea behind this is that the mackerel cannot then seize upon the trailing feathers and miss the hook altogether. Personally, I think this is a good idea if the feathers are bushy and extremely long, but I would be a bit cautious if the feathers are a bit sparse to begin with.

Whichever feathers you use, you will find, if you can afford it, that it is a good idea to have a telescopic rod made up ready with a trace. These rods are easy to store, perfectly adequate for the job and even come in handy if you decide to drop a set to the wreck and see what comes up. For myself I keep a DAM California 240, made up with a set of Hokkai lures and a miniature pirk weighing only a few ounces (60 g or so) instead of a weight. That way I am set up not just for catching bait, but also for having a bit of sport with cod, ling, pollack, spur-dogs and a variety of smaller fish.

Once you have caught your mackerel, you might as well leave them whole — and in the dark — until you get to the wreck. There you will have to decide whether to use them whole or filleted, cut into strips or mounted in one of a variety of ways. Your skipper should be able to give you a pretty good idea of what he expects to find, thereby enabling you to bait up accordingly, but as a rough guide you should find that strips are useful for bream, dogfish, spur-dogs and smaller species generally, while fillets are useful for rays, turbot, conger, ling, pollack, coalfish, cod and bass. Personally, I only use whole fish for shark, although some people do use them for conger. There is nothing wrong with this but I think it is more effective to remove the backbone, leaving two fillets still attached to the head. The hook should then rest in the mouth while the fillets are tied to the trace just above the eye of the hook. The advantage of this method is that you can lay up a much more effective scent trail because the blood is free to mingle with the current and entice the fish closer to the bait.

One last word of caution. Mackerel are not as common as they used to be. It is still possible to catch them in quantity if you happen to be in the right place at the right time, but it seems a great pity to slaughter large numbers when the chances are that you can catch enough to be going on with and then, later, catch a few more over the wreck where you will be fishing if you run short. Frankly, I have seen too many cases where the anglers on board a charter-boat catch far more mackerel than they need and end up killing a lot of fish unnecessarily. It is far better to take a responsible view and stop when you think you have enough, then top up with more on the wreck if you need to. That way we will all be helping to conserve the mackerel as a resource for future years instead of simply helping to deplete its dwindling stocks still further.

SQUID

Two types of squid are available to wreck-anglers: those native to our coastal waters and the smaller, imported *calamari*. The latter are by far the most commonly used as they are easy to get hold of, being packed in convenient boxes, frozen and sold in bulk through tackle shops and even some fishmongers. Being small, they can be used whole for species such as cod, for which they can be a deadly bait, or cut into strips for smaller fish, such as bream. They are readily obtainable, relatively inexpensive and effective for a variety of species. They are also fairly tough and stay on the hook very well, although their effectiveness is enhanced if you defrost them properly before you arrive on the wreck.

The larger squid that are found in British waters can be caught over most wrecks by using a squid jig on light tackle and working it close to the bottom. Jigs can be bought in most tackle shops and usually comprise a red elongated body made out of plastic with a double row of prongs at the bottom. As a jig is worked up and down in the water it entices a squid to attack; the squid is then caught on the prongs as it tries to reach the jig body. From here it can be swiftly brought to the surface but be wary, however, of the sepia ink which the squid can produce in copious amounts. Take a squid straight out of the water and you could find yourself setting an interesting fashion trend in clothes colour! The

The author with a pollack taken on the head of a calamari squid, often an effective bait when artificials fail to catch.

best thing to do is to net the squid and encourage it, at a safe distance, to get rid of its ink. When you think that there cannot be much left, swing it aboard, kill it humanely and cut it into long, tapering strips. Don't keep it alive in a bucket, as it can replenish its ink sacs in an amazingly short space of time!. You will also find, when you do cut it into strips, that you can increase your catch rate by peeling off the skin from the flesh. I don't really know why this works, but, in tests, nine out of ten cats said their dinners preferred it!

When you first catch a squid, you will notice that its colour tends towards pink rather than the more familiar white. This doesn't make any difference at all; the strips will bleach, so to speak, shortly after their owner's demise. If anything, the strips, as you might expect from really fresh bait, are more effective than defrosted frozen offerings.

You may find that there are occasions, while you are float-fishing from shore, when your float slowly disappears into the depths but, upon striking, instantly resurfaces with nothing being hooked. If this continues then the chances are that you have encountered either a squid or a cuttlefish, both of which will be very handy for wrecking. You may, if you are lucky, manage to hook one, but the chances are that you will not be so lucky unless you take extra steps to take it by surprise. The simplest way of doing this is to tie a small treble hook on a 6 in (150 mm) long trace to the bend of the hook upon which your bait has been mounted. When the squid seizes it, you should give it a few seconds to get a really good hold, then strike upwards firmly and quickly. The squid will be caught on the trailing treble and can be quickly pulled in, despatched, then stored for future use, sometimes giving a pretty good fight in the process!

An alternative method of getting hold of squid fairly cheaply is to approach a friendly fishmonger, or even the proprietor of a fish-and-chip shop. These individuals have access to a fishmarket and may be prepared, on a commission basis, to bid for a crate of English squid. Be prepared, however, to put your money up-front and make clear exactly what you are prepared to pay. That way the fishmonger knows what is going to be in it for him and you commit yourself only to a finite figure which you are sure you can afford. He makes a bit and you can, if you go about it the right way, save yourself quite a lot of money, especially if you split the cost between yourself and a few of your friends.

SAND-EELS

Several species of sand-eels inhabit British coastal waters, but it is only during the summer that large numbers of lesser and greater sand-eels come close enough to the shore to be netted on a regular basis and subsequently offered, alive, for sale. During this time, they are a first-class bait, although later, after they have once again moved out of the netsman's reach, you will find that frozen offerings have nowhere near the appeal of the live ones.

Sand-eels can be kept alive with an aerator and bucket, or in a livebait-troller that can be either home-made or shop-bought. Most skippers will have their own holder, or 'courge' as it is known, and will have established contacts to ensure that they can provide this excellent bait upon request. Generally, if you want live sand-eels, you can save yourself a lot of bother by simply making this known to the skipper in advance. Most will oblige you if they can, although they may, of course, charge extra for the privilege.

There are several ways of hooking sand-eels, but the method which I prefer is to pass the entire hook, point first, through the open mouth and out of the gills, then nick the stomach flesh lightly so that the hook is almost completely exposed. The eye will be clear of the mouth and gills while the trace, passing through both, will help to keep the sand-eels straight, both during the drop and upon the retrieve. Strips are not worth bothering with as they are very soft and easily removed from the hook, while at the same

A courge full of sand-eels, ideal for pollack, bass and a host of others.

time having far less attraction than a single live sand-eel. If you want to use strips for smaller species, then stick to either mackerel or squid. These are both superior to either dead or stripped sand-eels, although not as attractive as a well-presented live one.

PRAWNS

These lively crustaceans are not often used over wrecks but are a superb bait for a variety of species, including wrasse, bream, whiting, pout and bass. They are easy to catch in a drop net lowered from a harbour wall, or they can be hand-netted around rocks that are exposed during the low tide. Drop nets often take the biggest prawns but, for about 6 weeks in the summer, there are many rocky areas which suddenly seem to abound with large numbers of migratory prawns. During this period you can easily catch enough for a day with a few scoops of a suitable net, that is, a large one with a relatively small mesh and at least a 5 ft (1·5 m) handle. You will also find, amongst the catch, a large number of pregnant females. Please put these back.

Drop nets can be bought or made quite easily. Essentially they are a hoop, perhaps two hoops, which draws a small-meshed net into a circular shape roughly the size of a bicycle tyre. A piece of bait, perhaps the carcass of a mackerel, is tied to the middle of the net and the whole lowered into the water. Once a suitable depth has been selected, it is then left to attract any prawns in the immediate vicinity.

From time to time you will need to pull up and empty the net of any prawns that you have caught. You will also find large numbers of crabs, although none of them will be peelers. They are, however, still worth keeping, although not in the same container as the prawns. Keep a separate bucket handy, with some seaweed to throw over the ones that you catch. This will help to keep them moist and out of the sun. Even though they are hard-backed, they are still an excellent bait for big wrasse and smooth-hound.

Keep the water for the prawns well-aerated. Shakespeare offers an aerator which works off either batteries or a car battery via a transformer. This seems a good idea, but the aerator is expensive and does not, in my experience, have a longer working life than a normal aerator. To keep it in good working order, you will need to service it regularly, at the very least wiping down the outside connections after every trip and giving them a protective spray of WD40. You will also have to change the airstone, if not immediately then certainly after a few trips. This latter criticism, however, can be applied to all of the aerators which I have ever bought. Nowadays, I just throw away the one that comes with the pack, then replace it with a small wooden airstone. To prevent this floating to the surface, where its aeration would be ineffective, I encase it in a weighted swimfeeder with an enlarged central hole to take the plastic tubing that connects to the pump.

There does not seem to be a large selection of portable aerators on the market; only DAM and Shakespeare models spring to my mind from amongst the tackle manufacturers with which I am familiar. DAM, however, unlike Shakespeare, offers two aerators for use either with batteries or with a car battery via a plug that fits into the lighter socket of the car. It is worthwhile getting both because the battery model is useful for on board the boat while the 12 volt model saves money on batteries while the bait is in transit. There is not a lot of difference between the Shakespeare or DAM outfits with regard to price, but I have to admit that I would tend to opt for the two DAM aerators rather than the Shakespeare pump and its attendant transformer. However, whether you buy either of these or just a normal battery-powered aerator, it is worthwhile adding still another aerator to work off the mains in your house. The latter can be bought very cheaply, almost invariably from pet shops, and will soon save you more than enough money on batteries to justify its initial purchase. It is essential if you decide to set up a permanent tank for keeping live prawns, sand-eels or lugworms for any particular length of time. You will also need an under-gravel filter to keep the water clean and you will have to monitor closely the number of creatures which you put into the tank. Too many and the system will be unable to cope, so you might suffer some fatalities. The best thing to do is to ask for advice when you purchase the tank, aerator, etc., bearing in mind that the tank, if you want to use it for worms, will have to fit in a fridge as it is essential that the temperature is kept low enough to ensure their continued good condition. This is not as important for sand-eels or prawns, so you could get a much bigger tank for them.

To bait with prawns, you thread the point of the hook through the third segment from the tail, going from the underneath to the top. Some people like to use a hook with a very small gap, where the point is close to the shank of the hook, but I prefer a light-weight model with a fairly wide gap and a very short shank. This type does not interfere with the prawn's movement and presents the point well clear for the hooking of fish.

PEELER CRABS

For a crab to grow it needs first to develop a new, soft shell beneath the hard, older shell and then to shed the old shell and hide up for a few days while the new one hardens. During this process, crabs are first known as peeler crabs (before they shed the old shell) and, afterwards, as soft-backs. During both stages, they are extremely attractive and vulnerable to fish.

Anglers can use peeler crabs for a variety of species, from cod to bass, wrasse, pout, whiting, smooth-hound, flatfish and rays. It is an excellent and versatile bait, albeit expensive to buy and sometimes difficult to collect, especially during the winter months when it is in short supply. During the summer, when the warmer weather accelerates their metabolism and triggers the peeling process for huge

Collecting peeler crabs at low tide.

numbers of them, the crabs can be found by either hunting around rocks at low tide or diligently searching through weed and mud in favourable positions in estuaries.

To bait with peeler crab you will need some elasticated thread. Kill the crab humanely, then remove its claws and legs. Peel the shell from every part of the crab except one of the lower leg sockets. Pass the hook through the back, turn it, then thread it through and out of the bit of the shell that you left on the stump. Next cut a length of elasticated thread and tie the crab firmly to the hook. It does not matter if the crab gets squashed out of shape as this does not seem to make any difference to its

Peeler crabs make excellent bait but peeling edibles, by law, must be returned alive to the water.

attraction. When you have completed this stage, finish off by hanging a claw and a couple of legs from the point of the hook.

You don't have to use elasticated thread, but you will find that the bait lasts a lot longer if you do, because it is that much harder for any fish to rip it from the hook.

HERMIT CRABS

These are a much under-rated bait for a variety of species, provided that they are large enough to be interesting. They can be caught from the shore in a drop net lowered to the seabed in fairly deep water, especially if this is to a sandy bottom close to some rocks, but it is generally better to offer the crew of a crabbing vessel some money for saving you the hermits which get caught in their pots. This way is painless for you, although not for

them, and can easily get you enough bait to last a whole day and more.

To bait with hermits you first need to get them out of their shell. Heat the end of it slightly and they will either vacate the shell or die, in which case you can easily pull them free. General mayhem with a hammer is not recommended and can be incredibly messy, although it does seem to have its advocates. Once you have the hermit out, pass the hook once through the tough muscle with the tiny hooks at one end of the fluid-filled membrane. Slide this up and over the eye of the hook, which should be a fine wire Aberdeen (4/0 is a good size but this is clearly dependent upon the size of the crabs which you have caught), then turn the hook and pass the point once through the head. Do not puncture the body as this is the primary source of attraction.

LUGWORM

Lugworm, although not my favourite bait for any species save cod, are well worth a mention on that basis alone. There are days, both during the winter and the summer, when wrecks draw large numbers of these obliging and palatable fish. If you have lugworm handy then you can often make a very good catch. If you have not, then you can still take a few on mackerel fillets and peeler crab, not to mention live sand-eels and a whole *calamari* squid, but it is unlikely that you will catch as many.

Take a walk along any beach at low tide and the chances are that you will find some of the spiral casts that denote the presence of lugworm underneath. Look a bit closer and you will usually find a small breathing hole close to the main cast. Lying in a U-shaped tunnel connecting the two is the worm. If you excavate carefully, starting far enough back so as not to break the worm by stretching, you will soon find yourself getting expert at digging them up.

It does not usually take long to obtain enough for a day's outing, but you will find that you can dig a lot quicker if you follow the tide as it drops. Lugworm do not like having parched sand around them; consequently they go deeper as the tide goes further out. However, when the sand is first uncovered by the tide they are usually fairly close to the surface. If you take advantage of this, you can save yourself quite a lot of hard work.

Baiting with lugworm is not, I am afraid, a matter of finesse. Take three to six good-sized worms and thread them on a 4/0 to 6/0 Aberdeen, where they will make a very enticing bait for big cod. If you can get hold of some very thin rubber tubing, for example, the type used for holding line to the wire stems of pole floats, then you can use a length of this to slide up the hook and cover both the eye and the knot that you have tied. This not only protects the knot but also saves the worms from being lacerated by the nylon end which you trimmed.

Whatever bait you ultimately decide to use, one of those which I have mentioned or a different one altogether, such as ragworm, it will pay you to take some extra time to ensure that your bait is fresh and in tip-top condition. Try to bear in mind that, when you are fishing on a wreck, you are literally fishing 'in a land of plenty', for the wreck itself teems with a myriad offerings to both predators and prey. If you want your bait to be picked up, then it has to be up to scratch, that is, well presented and as fresh as possible. This means regularly changing the bait and always offering the best. If you don't do this, then you will jeopardize your chances of making that once-in-a-lifetime catch, the mysterious incentive which is far more likely on a wreck-fishing trip than on almost any other aspect of the sport.

Almost as bad is to put yourself in the position of relying upon a single bait. I have known trips where hours were wasted because no-one could get hold of any mackerel. That could have been avoided had a selection of other baits been brought on board, say squid, prawns and live sand-eels. You may also find that the fish do not respond to the particular bait which you either feathered or brought on board. This may be because they are feeding heavily upon a huge shoal of sand-eels or other small fish.

If the pickings are easy, then the local predators may start to gorge and become totally pre-occupied with the food that is on offer. If you cannot make the same offer then you might as well either close shop or appeal to a different sort of consumer. Having a variety of bait enables you to do just that, to change both your methods and display to bring the customers running. If you don't have variety, then you are limiting both your chances and your options. If you do – ah, well, then variety is the spice of life...

CHAPTER FOUR

SOME USEFUL KNOTS

There are many different types of knots which you can tie, but my concern in this chapter is not to provide an exhaustive and confusing list of alternatives, but to demonstrate clearly a few good knots with both words and pictures. To this end I am going to begin with the bimini hitch, a superb means of connecting any number of things to the line, then move on to the more conventional knots with which you may or may not already be acquainted. These will include the loop knot, which is invaluable for rigging paternoster-style tackles, the palomar and blood knots — for joining the line to pieces of terminal tackle, and the spool knot — for attaching the line to the spool of the reel. I will also demonstrate how to attach a hook or swivel to a length of wire using crimps, or to a piece of nylon-covered wire using the bimini hitch.

To make the bimini hitch you must first make a little tool (see diagram opposite) which will then probably last you for years. I made my first one 9 years ago and it is still going strong, despite being made out of an old coat-hanger, a piece of metal tubing, some dowel and a small amount of lead. These are fitted together in the following way. First cut a length of wire some 12 in (300 mm) long from the coat-hanger, then set this into a small piece of dowel, which is of the right diameter to fit tightly inside the metal tubing. Push the dowel to the bottom of the metal tube, which should be roughly 3 in (75 mm) long, so that it seals the end of the pipe. At this point, the wire will be passing up, and protruding from, the

middle of the tube. The next step is to melt the lead and fill the space above the dowel so that the wire is firmly trapped in place. A couple of kinks in the hidden length will make it doubly secure. The last stage is to bend the wire into the shape shown in the diagram, bending the last bit back a fraction to help the finished loop to slide easily from the tool. At this point you should carefully file away any rough edges so that there are no sharp parts to cut you when you spin the tool between your thumb and first two fingers. You will then be ready to tie your first loop.

To attach any tackle, you simply pass the line through it while it is held upon the tool. This will result in the swivel, hook, etc. being free-sliding upon the finished bimini loop. There is no chance of the knot strangling itself, that is, pulling itself tighter and tighter until the diameter becomes so thin that it cuts through itself, because the tackle *is* free-sliding. This gives you the full strength of the line, which has, in tests which I have carried out, almost always proved to be stronger than its stated breaking strain, probably as a result of the manufacturer's safety margin. It is a superb knot. However, despite years of telling people how good it is, it is still not in common use, which is a great pity. Having said that, there are a lot of converts who have seen me use it in action. The proof, it seems, is in the eating.

Do have a go. No other knot is anywhere near as reliable or as strong. If you know this knot you really, quite frankly, don't need any

BIMINI-HITCH TOOL

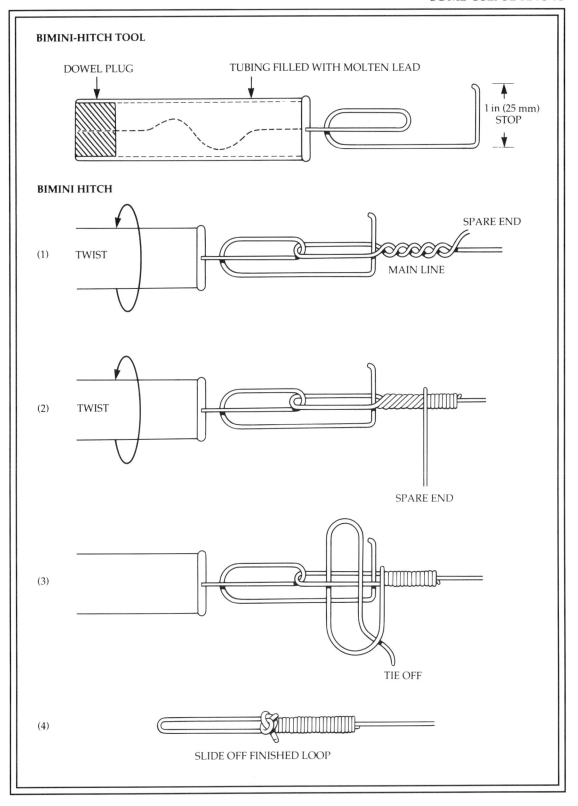

DOWEL PLUG

TUBING FILLED WITH MOLTEN LEAD

1 in (25 mm)
STOP

BIMINI HITCH

(1) TWIST

SPARE END

MAIN LINE

(2) TWIST

SPARE END

(3)

TIE OFF

(4)

SLIDE OFF FINISHED LOOP

other, although you will need a supply of oval links for joining traces to main line. If you do decide to have a go then this is how it is done. The set of diagrams on page 45 will help you get it right.

Slide the line through the eye of the tool, passing it through any piece of tackle that you want included on the loop. Double it back so that it passes itself on the opposite side of the stop, this being sandwiched between the main line and the end that you are using to tie the knot. Pull tight on the line and begin to twist the tool. The end and the line will begin to wrap together. Allow this to happen to the desired length, which should not be less than $\frac{3}{4}$ in (20 mm), depending upon the diameter of the line, then stop the end so that it turns back towards the tool. Guide it so that it coils tightly and neatly about the twisted strands, working it gradually downwards until it comes to rest at the stop on the tool. The distance between the eye and the stop will determine the size of the loop. Obviously this is fixed when the tool is made, so if you want different sizes of loops then you will have to make such tools as you deem appropriate.

When the coils come to rest against the stop, perform the finishing knots. There are three of these to tie. All you have to do, keeping the line tight all the time, is to pass the spare end up between the two strands of line that are held on the tool, making a loop to one side of the stop. Pass the end through the loop, making sure that it doesn't get stuck around the stop, then pull it tight. Repeat this on the opposite side of the stop, then back on the original side for the final knot. Pull it as tight as you can without breaking the line, then trim it and hold it up in the air. The tool will spin for a few moments, losing any potential twists, and you should then wet your thumb and forefinger and draw them slowly down the line, encouraging any final kinks to depart. Then, and only then, can you let the line go slack. Do it earlier and you will have a massive tangle. The last thing to do is to pull the knot up and over the stop, then

simply slide it around the wire and free from the tool.

The diagrams should help to make the process clear. However, if you are working in nylon-covered wire, you will have to take steps to prevent any kinks at all from forming. This is done by cutting a length slightly in excess of the desired trace and roughly tying one end to a swivel. The swivel is hung over a cup hook and the bimini hitch tied to the other end as before, only this time the wire is periodically relaxed just a trifle to allow the swivel to spin and stop any kinks from forming. Once you have finished one end, then you simply cut off the swivel and attach it to the completed loop with an oval link. Repeat the process so that you have a perfect bimini hitch at each end of the trace, perhaps with a hook upon one and a swivel or link upon the other. This method of attachment is far and away stronger than using crimps, but it is only practicable up to approximately 45 lb (20·4 kg) breaking strain in nylon-covered wire, or up to 120 lb (54·4 kg) breaking strain in nylon monofilament. This is, however, as much as you could ever possibly need, even though you may have to pull the ends tight with a pair of pliers for maximum security. You cannot put 45 lb (20·4 kg) of pressure on a fish with a rod. It is not possible. Nor is a fish able to bite through the wire, except, perhaps, shark, for which you will need to use much heavier wire and attach tackle using crimps (this method is demonstrated in the set of diagrams on page 52).

The set of diagrams opposite shows you how to tie a stand-off loop. This is a useful knot both for making up conventional paternosters and also for changing and attaching lures. Some people, when they are putting paternosters together, trim one strand of the loop very close to the main line, resulting in a longer trace to which you can tie a hook as normal. Others, following the same sort of logic as myself, don't cut the loop, but simply slide it through the eye of a hook, loop it over the point and bend, then draw it back until it

STAND-OFF LOOP

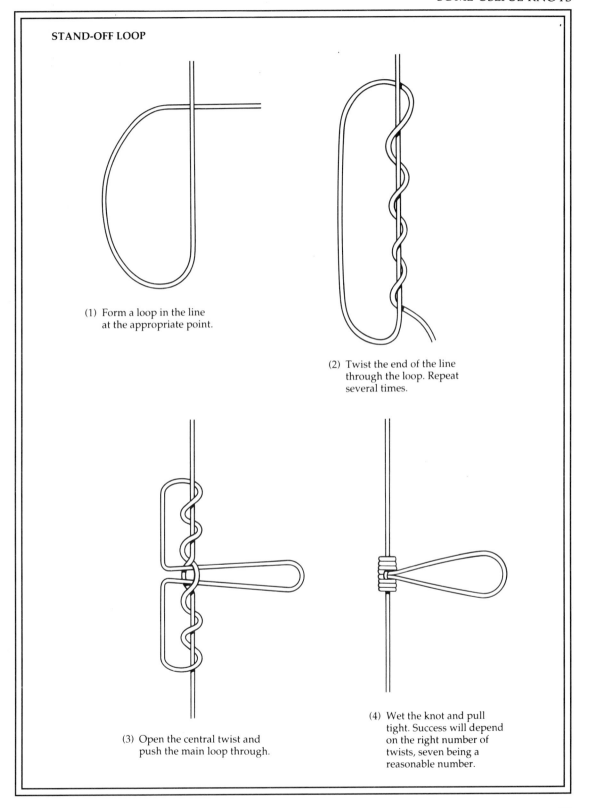

(1) Form a loop in the line at the appropriate point.

(2) Twist the end of the line through the loop. Repeat several times.

(3) Open the central twist and push the main loop through.

(4) Wet the knot and pull tight. Success will depend on the right number of twists, seven being a reasonable number.

cannot go any further. At this point the hook is firmly attached, additional pressure only drawing it tighter. There is no knot as such, hence no danger of the line being cut through strangulation. Furthermore, the hook is supported not by one, but by two strands of line. To change the hook or lure is also simplicity itself. You simply reverse the process, easing the tension on the line so that you can free the loop and draw it back through the eye of the hook.

You may worry that the two strands of line make the short trace appear bulky and off-putting to the fish. Frankly, that doesn't really matter if you are going after the larger species. The rubber bodies of artificial eels will render the problem negligible for pollack, while the sheer scale of baits intended for cod or ling will almost certainly wipe out any pressing need for finesse. Add to this the fact that little light penetrates to the bottom in deeper water, meaning that there will be little chance of the fish spotting the double strands, and you can see that the advantages of strength and quick changing of lures will outweigh the minimal handicap of any reduction in subtlety. The only species for which I might make an exception is bream, but even then I may not bother, especially if I have already reduced the strength of my main line to match the much lighter tackle that I would be using at the time.

The next set of diagrams (opposite) shows you how to tie a palomar knot, a useful enough knot but one which suffers from the drawback that it can only be used to attach one eye of a swivel and not both. It also tends to be a trifle erratic with regard to strength. In tests, it has been demonstrated that most palomars offer a high percentage of the line's stated breaking strength, say between 80 and 90 per cent; then, for no apparent reason, an odd knot comes along which snaps at under 50 per cent, literally halving the strength of your line. For this reason, it is always best to check every knot that you tie. Most of the time it will be a very strong, reliable knot that will not let you down, but at other times it

may, so it is best to check. You also have the problem of the other eye of that swivel; to deal with this, I have included a set of diagrams and explanatory text on the blood knot (see page 50).

The last set of diagrams in this chapter are of the spool knot (page 51), for attaching your main line to the spool of your reel, and a method of attaching wire line to a piece of tackle using crimps (page 52). There are no particular problems with the spool knot, which is, after all, a fairly simple knot, but you can get problems with crimping wire line, the most common being simple heavy-handedness. For the join to be effective, you must take care not to exert too much pressure on the crimping ferrules (crimps for short) when you close them on the wire line. You have to be firm, certainly, but you don't want to be heavy-handed. I have seen people straining away at the job with the inevitable result that they damage both the crimps and the line. The best thing to do is to be careful while you make the join, exerting a firm but controlled pressure on the crimps, then test the finished result to see if it stands up to pressure. If it does, then you have nothing to worry about. If it doesn't, then simply repeat the join, this time exerting just that little extra bit of pressure to ensure a solid grip. Also bear in mind that you will need pliers to do the job properly, so don't leave them ashore if you have no traces made up in advance of your trip.

Between them, the knots that I have mentioned will cover most of the eventualities that you are likely to face. Purists may say that I have not demonstrated how to join two lines together but, quite frankly, that is purely because I don't think such knots have a place in wreck fishing. They so reduce the strength of the line that a fish of any size may quite easily break it. That would be a great pity if that particular fish was a record-breaker to boot. Don't take chances with either your knots or your main line. Make sure that they are both up to standard and that neither will

PALOMAR KNOT

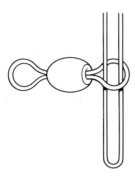

(1) Double 6 in (150 mm) of line back on itself. Push both strands through the eye of the swivel or hook.

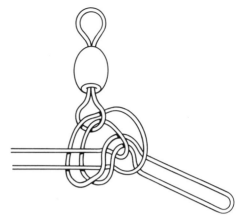

(2) Tie an overhand knot, leaving a loop big enough to pass over the item being tied.

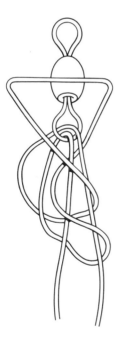

(3) Pass the loop over the item and draw it gently down pulling the knot tight as you do so.

(4) Fully tighten the knot, making sure that the coils bed evenly as you pull.
Trim the spare end fairly closely and check that the knot is secure.

BLOOD KNOT

(1) Push the line through the eye and double it back.

(2) Begin to twist the spare end around the main line.

(3) Repeat this several times according to the diameter of the line.

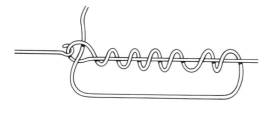

(4) Tuck the spare end through the first loop next to the eye.

(5) Pull tight and trim.

VARIATION: TUCKED BLOOD KNOT

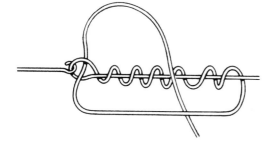

Turn the spare end through the big loop that was formed at stage 4. Pull tight and trim. Stages 1 to 3 are exactly the same.

SPOOL KNOT

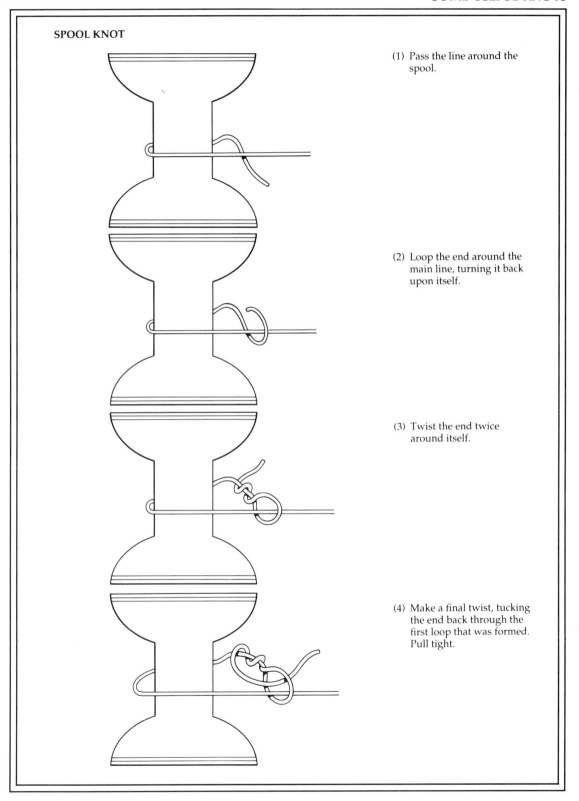

(1) Pass the line around the spool.

(2) Loop the end around the main line, turning it back upon itself.

(3) Twist the end twice around itself.

(4) Make a final twist, tucking the end back through the first loop that was formed. Pull tight.

USING CRIMPS FOR WIRE LINE

(1) Pass the wire through the eye of the swivel or hook.

(2) Make a couple of turns through the eye and lay the spare end alongside the main.

(3) Slide on the first crimping ferrule (crimp for short) and close it fully. Trim the spare end and slide on a second crimp which will then effectively shroud any protruding sharp points.

(4) Alternatively, double the spare end back and trap it beneath the first crimp. The second crimp then traps the resulting loop, shrouding it for neatness and to prevent tangles.

let you down. If the day ever comes when a really big fish takes your bait, and with wreck-fishing there is always a good chance of this happening, then you will have the confidence to be able to play that fish to the limits of both your skill and your strength. If you are worried about your knots, then you will never take either to their limits. The fish will not be subject to these restrictions. It will do its best to get away, either breaking your line or taking you into the wreck, where the best you can do is to pull for a break. So, at the end of the day, your knots may be the most expensive part of your tackle. They may not cost any money, but they might cost you the fish of a lifetime – or they may help you to bring it aboard. In the final analysis, tying good knots might be far more important than you initially suppose, so it is well worth taking a little extra time and effort to do them well. Your reward might be greater than you think.

CHAPTER FIVE

POLLACK AND COALFISH

There are few things more thrilling than the first, tremendous dive of a hooked pollack. One moment you are reeling in the lure, the next second you are stopped dead in the retrieve as a well-muscled fish, weighing anything from 2–30 lb (1–14 kg), seizes it and turns for the bottom. At that moment, if you lock up against the fish, then the chances are that you will lose it. On the other hand, you can give it a few seconds with your drag set so that it can take line off under pressure, then, when its impetus fades, you can apply extra pressure and turn it from its intended destination: the wreck with its shelter and masts so close at hand.

If you fail, and if the fish reaches shelter with your line trailing in its wake, then the chances are that you will end up pulling for a break against whatever obstruction the fish has wrapped your line around. Not only that, but you may have tethered the fish to the spot, where it stands very little chance of survival. It is therefore imperative that your tackle is well up to the job. Any weakness will soon be found out, almost certainly the hard way.

That doesn't mean that your tackle should be so stiff and heavy that a pollack doesn't have much of a chance. If you use 50 lb (22·7 kg) class tackle, for example, then you will soon find that the fish are almost completely outgunned. The only exception to this is if you are using a multi-hook tackle designed to catch more than one at a time which, although it catches numbers of fish,

doesn't really make for an interesting day. After all, what you are doing is simply dragging them to the surface on tackle which has been designed not to be broken. The resulting fight is limited and the winching up resembles hard work more than angling. It is far better to stick to lighter tackle, say up to 30 lb (13·6 kg) class maximum, and use only one lure or one hook at a time. For myself I prefer to use an uptide boatcaster matched with a reel like the Shimano Triton Charter and loaded with 25 lb (11·3 kg) breaking strain line. This is heavy enough to deal with a hard-fighting coalfish, should one take the lure, but light enough to enjoy every stage of the fight. The longer rod is also useful for controlling the fish. The tip cushions any sudden dives and stops the line from breaking, while the rod is still sufficiently powerful to turn the fish long before it can tangle itself in the wreck.

Some anglers like to use 12 or 20 lb (5·4 or 9·1 kg) tackle when they are going for pollack. The same comments apply for the 20 lb (9·1 kg) class as for the uptide boatcaster, although the longer length of the boatcaster will give you a bit more control. 12 lb (5·4 kg) class is, if you will excuse the pun, a different kettle of fish. It is perfectly capable of handling the majority of pollack, but it calls for considerable skill if you suddenly find yourself tangling with a 25 lb (11·3 kg) coalfish. These fight a lot harder than pollack, putting such a strain upon both tackle and angler that newcomers to wreck angling would be very lucky to eventually bring them aboard. It is certainly

Pumping a large fish with the rod tucked under the arm.

a sporting way of catching bigger fish, but I would seriously suggest that beginners become familiar with slightly heavier outfits first and then, when they have developed some skill at playing fish, move to the lighter outfits if they want to.

On a good day's pollacking, the lucky angler can find himself tiring from pulling up fish after fish from whatever depths the wreck is lying in. As you can imagine that calls for a considerable amount of exertion. It is bad enough on light tackle but, on heavy gear, pulling three up at a time, it is extremely hard work, especially if there are bigger fish around. A butt pad (see Chapter 1) can at least prevent your groin from becoming sore, but there are many people who prefer to fight the fish with the rod tucked under the arm. This is fine for light tackle, where the position facilitates the

rod's ability to contend with sudden dives, but it is better, if you are using stronger rods, to use a butt pad for the support it can offer. That way you can really bend into fish without suffering too much discomfort.

A lot of people, used to the longer butts of beachcasters, make the mistake of trying to tuck the butt in between their legs. This is inefficient and painful. After all, on a beachcaster you are contending with a fish at quite a distance from the shore and there is a considerable angle between you and the fish, enabling your arms to take the majority of the strain while your legs prevent the butt from flopping around. On a wreck, the fish are right below the rod tip, pulling down as opposed to pulling away. As you can imagine, if they are pulling down the tip, then your arms, supporting the reel, will act as a pivot so that there is some pressure on the butt to come up. With a big fish that pressure is considerable, so you can imagine what a sudden lunge can do to your privates if you are taken unawares!

Multi-hook tackle usually consists of either feathers, feathers plus a pirk, several rubber eels, or eels plus a pirk. If you want to use this type of tackle then you will find little difference in their performance, but the addition of a pirk will occasionally bring other species, such as ling or cod, to the boat. However, I would suggest that you never put on more than three hooks at any one time so, if you are using a pirk, that would count as one, enabling you to fish only two lures above it. If you catch a fish on both eels and the pirk then believe me, you will know about it. You will also find that there is considerable pressure put upon the line out of which your tackle is tied, especially with three feathers or eels, in which case you

might find three very large fish pulling in opposite directions. On lighter line, the strain is simply too much. The angler feels at first one then possibly two decided changes in the weight that he is bringing aboard. What has happened is that first one and then another lure has come adrift from the trace. To prevent this happening, you need to tie any feathers or multi-lure rigs out of very strong nylon. Personally, although it is not a method I often use, I tie mine out of 100 lb (45·4 kg) breaking strain monofilament, connecting it by a strong swivel and the bimini hitch to 50 lb (22·7 kg) main line. The resultant tackle will handle just about anything that is thrown at it, but is a little too unsporting for my taste. However, having said that, one has to appreciate that wreck trips are expensive. Many anglers will therefore want to fill a large part of their freezers to help to defray the cost. On some

A 9 lb (4 kg) pollack from a wreck lying close inshore.

boats, the skipper will even offer the anglers a share in the proceeds from selling any surplus catch at a fishmarket. In both cases, many anglers would feel perfectly justified – and quite rightly – in using such a tackle. It is therefore illustrated on page 58.

You will notice that two strands of line are indicated as passing into the body of the eel. This is because there are two ways of using dropper loops to fasten a lure. One is to slide on the body of the lure, pushing it well up the trace, then push the loop through the eye of the hook and loop it over the point. When you pull on the line this slides up the shank and secures the eel firmly in place, the body being moved down to cover the hook. The second method is to tie a dropper loop and then cut one strand of the loop next to the main line, using this to tie on the lure in the normal way. Personally, I only use this second method when I want the lure to have a lot of movement. For Redgills or feathers on this kind of tackle it is not really necessary, but if you were using muppets for cod then the longer traces would be advantageous.

If you want to use feathers then I would suggest that you tie your own. Commercial ones are all very well, but in the larger sizes they tend to be white. They catch fish, but they don't catch as many as other colours tied in a more interesting way. Personally I prefer to use feathers that have been dyed red, yellow or black (not that yellow is a particularly successful colour for pollack, but it will bring aboard the occasional cod, which I am sure would not come as too much of a disappointment). I also like to match these with some rubber tubing, tying the feathers first, then sliding on a rubber body where one side of the tube has been cut away to make a long, tapering tail. You can go to a lot of effort over these lures or you can do them simply and cheaply. I prefer to put the feathers roughly into position and then whip them to the shank of the hook, sealing the whipping thread with a touch of varnish, leaving it to dry and then hiding that part within the

rubber body as I have already mentioned. This is simple and effective, catching a number of fish and being very inexpensive. Also, if you are like me, then it will give you a great deal of pleasure to catch fish on lures that you have made yourself.

If you have not done a whipping before, then the set of diagrams on page 59 should enable you to see how it is done. This is exactly the same method that you would use for attaching a ring to your rod, should you have the misfortune to have one come astray. Full instructions are given in the diagrams.

As far as the pirk is concerned, you will find it more comfortable to fish with the lightest possible than simply to stick on a big one and work it through the whole of the tide, which is both cumbersome and tiring. It is far better to carry a selection of pirks in different sizes so that you can keep scaling down as the current drops. If you use a light enough model you can also drop it down to the bottom, bounce it, simultaneously letting out a few feet ($\frac{1}{2}$ a metre or so) of line, then repeat the process, gradually working the lure away from its first point of descent until it comes in contact with the fish. The thing to watch out for is that you really are bouncing the lure away and not just letting out slack line to form a great belly that tangles with other people's lines. You will, therefore, need to hold the spool tight between every drop, feel the current take the lure and then be sensitive to the slight jar as it touches the bottom. If you cannot feel this, then the pirk is just sitting there while the current takes your line, in which case you need to reel in until you once again establish contact. You may also find that the fish are not feeding on the bottom, so you will need to concentrate on jigging the tackle at different levels until the fish are found.

Over the years I have usually found that pollack respond better to a small pirk than a big one. You can still make your own, but an excellent range of stainless-steel jiggers is available from Ryobi. They are not cheap, but they are good, with a range of weights to

POLLACK: MULTI-HOOK TACKLE

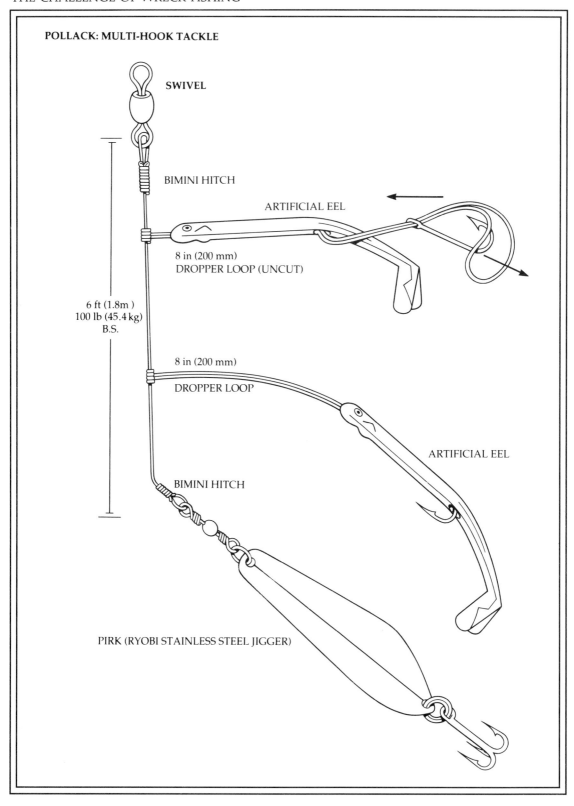

SWIVEL

BIMINI HITCH

ARTIFICIAL EEL

8 in (200 mm)
DROPPER LOOP (UNCUT)

6 ft (1.8m)
100 lb (45.4 kg)
B.S.

8 in (200 mm)
DROPPER LOOP

ARTIFICIAL EEL

BIMINI HITCH

PIRK (RYOBI STAINLESS STEEL JIGGER)

HOW TO MAKE YOUR OWN LURES FOR POLLACK

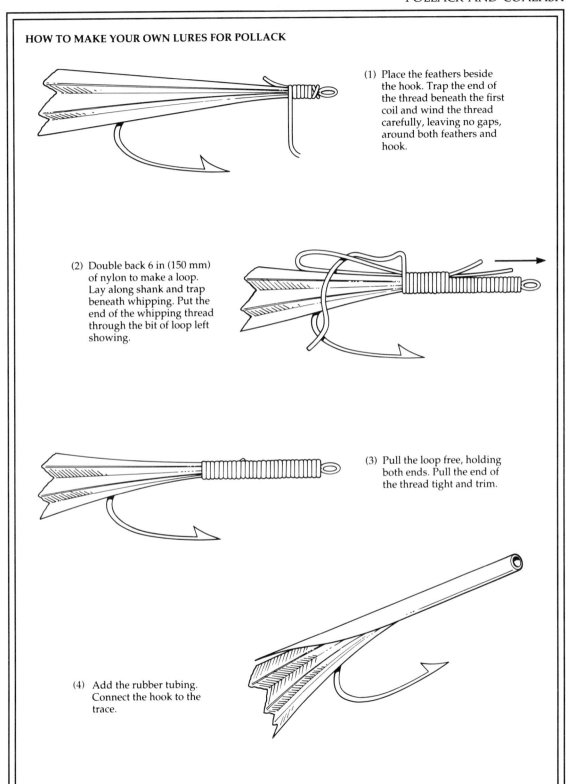

(1) Place the feathers beside the hook. Trap the end of the thread beneath the first coil and wind the thread carefully, leaving no gaps, around both feathers and hook.

(2) Double back 6 in (150 mm) of nylon to make a loop. Lay along shank and trap beneath whipping. Put the end of the whipping thread through the bit of loop left showing.

(3) Pull the loop free, holding both ends. Pull the end of the thread tight and trim.

(4) Add the rubber tubing. Connect the hook to the trace.

cater for almost every situation which you are likely to encounter. Their slightly curved shape also gives them a slight fluttering motion which is particularly attractive on the descent.

One thing you will find is that you won't catch many coalfish by this method; most seem to be caught on single Redgills worked on a flowing trace as shown in the diagram opposite. If you do catch one, then you can distinguish it from pollack by the fact that the jaws are roughly level (the pollack's lower jaw protrudes) and the lateral line is straight (in the case of the pollack it curves slightly over the pectoral fin – the one on the side, just behind the head). Coloration is fairly similar in both, especially after death, while I fancy that the coalfish makes slightly better eating.

There are quite a few lures which you can use for pollack, but pride of place must certainly go to Redgill or Eddystone lures. Different colours will catch on different days, but the ones most worth examining are black, red, red-and-black combinations, grey, fluorescent-orange and red-and-orange combinations. These may seem like personal choice, but a few years ago, while working on my degree, I made these lures the subject of a very detailed statistical analysis for my independent study. To make this in any way comprehensive, I was fortunate enough to be sent a full range of lures from both Eddystone and Redgill, which I supplemented with other models purchased at the time. All of these lures were then subjected to a considerable number of tests – over 5,000 separate drops – to see if any colours performed better than any others. I was also testing to see what effect, if any, size of lure made upon the resultant size of fish caught. A drift which failed to put a fish on board the deck was not counted as there may, hypothetically, have been no fish around at that particular moment. Despite this, however, at the end of my tests there were still over 3,000 acceptable results upon which to base my analysis; amongst other things, this highlighted the above colours as being the most

effective for pollack and demonstrated that the average size of fish definitely increased with any increase in the size of lure. Coalfish, funnily enough, didn't make much of an appearance but, where they did so, it seemed as if their preference was for smaller black eels. They didn't show during the tests but, to counter this, I was also monitoring and recording all captures of pollack and coalfish that were reported in the fishing newspapers. From these reports, it became clear that the smaller black eels were accounting for more than their fair share of coalfish.

Some other lures which are worth examining are the Roland Martin spinners. Designed initially for small-mouthed bass, these lures are fast proving themselves to be deadly for pollack, although I have yet to catch a coalfish on one. They are also accounting for other species, such as cod and ling, and are showing such promise that I would not be surprised to see some anglers using them in preference to artifical eels. Seeing these in action made me wonder whether a home-made lure, utilizing an artificial eel, might be similarly productive. Accordingly I used the bimini hitch to make the tackle shown in the diagram on 62. The Roland Martin spinners utilize a small, fast-vibrating spoon, but I decided to investigate the effect of increasing the size of the spoon and changing its shape so as to slow down significantly the number of rotations. The results have been good, certainly more than enough to justify continued research, but I would like to see a lot more people experimenting along these lines before I make any kind of comparison between this and other lures. It has certainly performed well enough to give it a go, although, if you decide to look into this for yourself, I would definitely recommend experimenting with the size, colour and shape of the spoon. In the end, it could surprise you. A point which always springs to my mind is an old book by Herbert Jenkins, writing under the pseudonym of Seangler, entitled *Flatfish and How to Catch Them*. In this small book, essentially an exhaustive

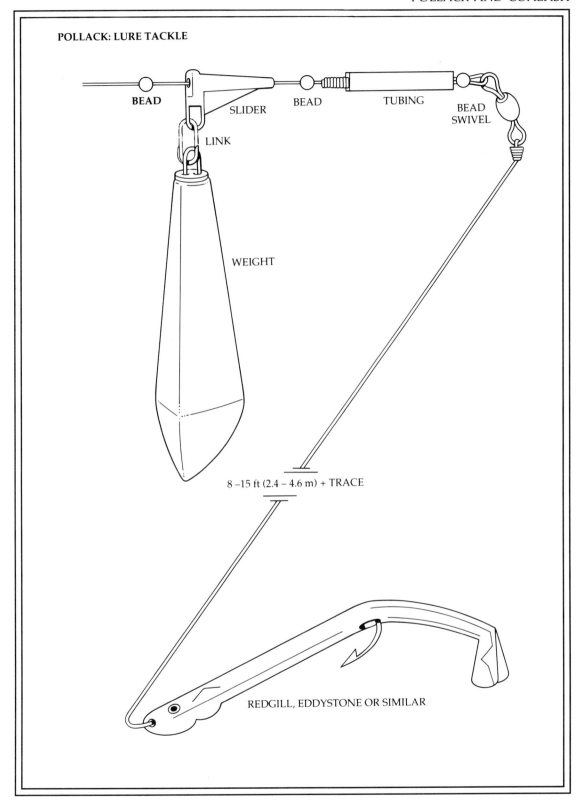

POLLACK: LURE TACKLE

BEAD

SLIDER

BEAD

TUBING

BEAD
SWIVEL

LINK

WEIGHT

8 –15 ft (2.4 – 4.6 m) + TRACE

REDGILL, EDDYSTONE OR SIMILAR

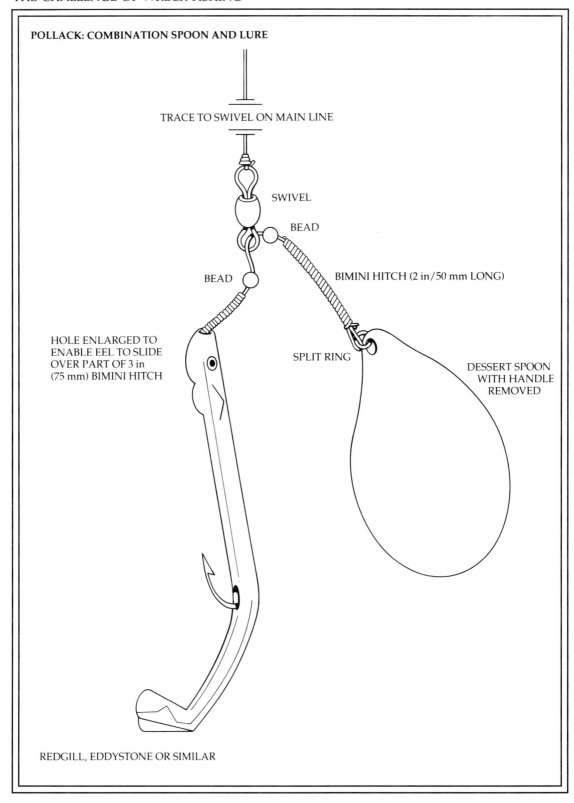

POLLACK: COMBINATION SPOON AND LURE

TRACE TO SWIVEL ON MAIN LINE

SWIVEL

BEAD

BEAD

BIMINI HITCH (2 in/50 mm LONG)

HOLE ENLARGED TO
ENABLE EEL TO SLIDE
OVER PART OF 3 in
(75 mm) BIMINI HITCH

SPLIT RING

DESSERT SPOON
WITH HANDLE
REMOVED

REDGILL, EDDYSTONE OR SIMILAR

discussion of using the baited spoon, a popular method for flatfish which he pioneered, the author quite categorically states that spoons in excess of $4\frac{1}{2}$ in (114 mm) length were very attractive to pollack. Bearing this in mind, I have to admit to a certain curiosity about how such spoons will perform with the combination tackle I am currently testing. Unfortunately I have not yet found any metal spoons of the right size and shape, that is, where the spoon doesn't thicken towards the handle but maintains a uniform thickness of metal, enabling the angler to hacksaw off the handle and round the spoon to ensure that its action is consistent. If you can get hold of such a spoon then you might find yourself with a really winning combination. I cannot say for certain, but I think it is well worth having a go.

Apart from these lures, there are a number of latex models coming on the market, particularly ones imported from the USA. These are gradually acquiring a small number of converts, but to date I have not seen them perform sufficiently well to overcome my preference for artificial eels. The ones which come nearest are available in a range of colours and dimly resemble a lugworm with a curved tail. The only disadvantage with these is that they contain some sort of inhibitor to prevent the latex from becoming dry and perished. I discovered this when I removed them from a plastic container only to find that they had almost melted their way out. Consequently I was compelled to keep them apart from my usual lures in a small metal tin kept expressly for the purpose.

If you don't want to use lures at all, and many people don't, then you can substitute a plain hook for the lure and simply fish with either a long mackerel strip, say a fillet cut in half lengthways, or a live sand-eel. The sand-eel is probably the best, but you will occasionally find it being taken by smaller fish, such as pout. The best thing to do is to see if the netters will keep some of the bigger launce (another name for the greater sand-eel, which grows to a much larger size than the lesser sand-eel) until you have the time to collect them. These can measure in excess of 12 in (300 mm) and seem to discourage the smaller fish. On the other hand they are also accepted by both ling and bass, although I am sure you will not be discouraged if you find a double-figure bass turning up on your line. However, to be quite frank, I don't think that any natural bait will perform so well as an artificial eel if the fish are really on the feed. There is something about them, most probably the vibrations, which can be almost overwhelmingly attractive to pollack. Natural bait, although it takes its fair share, doesn't seem to have anywhere near the same appeal, which, if you think about it, is not really surprising. A lure arrives at the bottom in the same condition as it leaves the top. A live sand-eel, plummeting quickly to a great depth, invariably suffers. Retrieve them side by side and the lure, sending out its 'come and get me' signals, will almost always catch more fish, at least as long as you have chosen a sensible colour.

When you do get a pollack on board, you will often find that its swim-bladder, unable to contend with rapid changes in pressure, has erupted through its intestine and lodged in its mouth. There is no point in prolonging its agony, as it has no chance of survival, so the humane and practical thing to do is to kill it quickly and store it safely in the dark of the fish-hold. The same goes for coalfish, which can also suffer, though not to the same extent as pollack.

One last thing I should mention is that there is always, with these particular species, a reasonable chance of breaking the British record, something which has happened quite a few times in recent years. However, this chance would seem to be greatest during the period from January to March. This is the time during which the fish are congregating on the wrecks and packing on weight in the expectation of spawning, rapidly approaching their maximum weight for the particular year. Consequently, trips at this time can be very rewarding, but are often uncomfortable due to

A brace of southern pollack from a mark, scarcely 500 yd (458 m) from the shore.

heavy seas or bitingly cold weather. The quantity of fish caught would seem to make the endurance of such conditions worthwhile but, at the end of the day, when you are relaxing in a nice hot bath, perhaps easing muscles sorely tried from their exertions against hard-fighting coalfish, it will pay you, even if you were successful, to review both your tactics and performance to see how you can better your chances.

And what happens if you were not successful? Just do exactly the same: try to work out where you went wrong, then determine that next time is going to be *the* trip that makes it all worthwhile. It may well prove to be just that, for I have often found that a positive attitude encourages success, particularly in wreck fishing, where the unknown, like the pollack, is waiting in ambush and may even take the shape of a potential British record.

CHAPTER SIX

COD

As the sun finally broke through the clouds, dispelling the illusion that autumn had come early, so the skipper, after 3 hours of steaming, throttled back on his engines and brought the boat almost completely to a stop. For a moment there was confusion as everybody seized part of the boat to hold on to, overtaken as we were by the wash from the vessel itself. Then 12 pairs of eyes turned expectantly towards the cabin and the individual watching the instruments within.

Silence reigned as people carefully picked up their rods, making last-minute checks of their tackle to ensure that all was in order. There followed an abrupt, chopping motion of the skipper's hand, combined with the crew calling gleefully 'There's plenty of fish!' and 12 sets of tackle plummetted from the sides and swiftly vanished into the mysterious waters below, carrying with them both our hopes and our raised expectations. Each of us were tense, feeling that surge of excitement and anticipation which, for me and nearly all of my friends, never fails to visit us on the first drop of each trip.

One angler grinned, quirking his eyebrows as he waited for his tackle to reach the bottom. He gave the impression that, had his hands not been full, he must surely have rubbed them together. His mood was infectious, with smiles and soft laughs, strangely muted, to show that we too knew just how he felt.

An angler to the right of me stiffened, sensitive to the impact far below as his tackle reached the bottom. With quiet confidence he dropped the rod tip, turned the handle of the reel as he made contact with the weight, then began a steady retrieve as he drew his orange Redgill upwards through the water.

Watching him, totally oblivious to anything but his tackle, I nodded as he stopped winding after a couple of minutes, then released the spool so that once again his lure sought the bottom and the fish that he expected to find. He looked up, surprised to find me watching, then grinned as his rod tip abruptly bounced, then drew downwards in steady pulls, for all the world as if some creature far below was nodding its tacit agreement.

'It's a nodder!' cried one of the crew, a hairy and rather fragrant individual given to these short, cryptic utterances. Then, as if exhausted by the effort, he relapsed into silence, pulling about him an air of gloomy dejection, only partially relieved by the sudden brilliance of his smile as he reached for the gaff, extending it swiftly so that it almost seemed to stroke the side of the great cod that now appeared from the depths.

The crew man pursed his lips, conveying silently by contortions his unreserved appreciation of its size and beautiful proportions — this mottled giant weighing in excess of 20 lb (9 kg). Once again he nodded to its beaming captor, then lapsed into dejection as he dropped it back over the side.

You could have heard a pin drop in the silence that followed. Its captor opened his mouth, then, as if nothing forceful enough could emerge from his stupefaction, he simply closed it and turned towards the skipper for an explanation.

'Cod ban', was the gloomy answer to his unspoken question. 'Got to put it back. Them too!' A hand thus disposed of three more beautiful fish. 'Change your eels. Put on some black, take off any orange or yellow or white.' Grimly, he turned to oversee the return of the other fish, then clapped a shoulder in mute apology and sympathy as the unfortunate angler complied with his instruction.

On this particular day, we had steamed over 20 miles (32 km) from port in the expectation of some good pollack. Only a few of these appeared, drawn almost invariably by red, black or red-and-black lures, but we seemed to have been positioned over a wreck teeming with cod. Despite our change of lures, still more and more fish appeared until the skipper, growing more anguished with every fish that had to be returned, decided that enough was enough and moved us to a different wreck.

On this occasion, we were unfortunate enough to be adversely affected by a hastily-conceived and generally-imposed cod ban. Since then, such bans have come and gone with monotonous regularity, although it now appears that many angling boats may be excepted from having to comply with their directive. Had it not been for the ban we would, headed out from a southern port as we were, have counted ourselves extremely fortunate to have encountered such fish. Most of us would have expected to have travelled north to such areas as Whitby to meet cod in such quantity and size, even as many northern anglers would have expected to come south to meet similar quantities of pollack and coalfish.

Our tackle had been determined by pollack, most of us using the lure tackle illustrated in Chapter 5. Had we been deliberately after cod, then our methods may have been more varied, with quite a few more muppets in evidence than eels.

Muppets are basically latex squid. They are available in a range of colours, from purples and blues – which I have yet to see catch a fish – to such favourites as yellow, orange and white. They are not overly expensive, catch a lot of fish and are also useful for adorning the large treble hooks situated at the bottom of pirks. They are also quite easy to make out of rubber tubing.

My favourites are made out of the white rubber tubes which are found on milk-vending packs. Thousands of these are daily thrown away from cafés and restaurants throughout the UK, so I duly found a receptive patron and politely asked if some could be saved. From that casual request I was later able to make some two dozen lures at a cost of a few words and absolutely no money.

If you look at the diagram on page 68, you will see just how easy these are to make. All you need is a steady hand and a pair of scissors. It is, however, worthwhile to experiment with the proportions of each lure. A 2 in (50 mm) head is extremely useful for covering a 6/0 O'Shaugnessy, such as you might be working off a dropper loop above a pirk, but a 1 in (25 mm) head is better if the muppet is to be used on a treble hook. Probably the best answer is to make up a selection, not only of sizes, but of colours, looking at the different tubes available in such fields as home-brewing, siphoning or whatever other avenues your own ingenuity may suggest.

There are three main methods of catching cod. Lure-fishing I have already mentioned, but pirking and legering also deserve serious consideration.

If we look at pirking first, there are several methods of actually rigging the tackle, although the main methods are single pirk at the end of the line, perhaps with either a muppet, a real *calamari* squid or a fillet of mackerel as bait, or a pirk with a multi-hook rig such as that described in Chapter 5 for pollack. Which you use will depend on whether you want to put quality of sport over quantity of catch, although that is not quite as simple as it sounds because, if fish are scarce, multi-hook tackle may attract more cod to it

COD: HOME-MADE MUPPETS

REMOVE 2 in (50 mm) SECTION FROM 6 in (150 mm) LENGTH

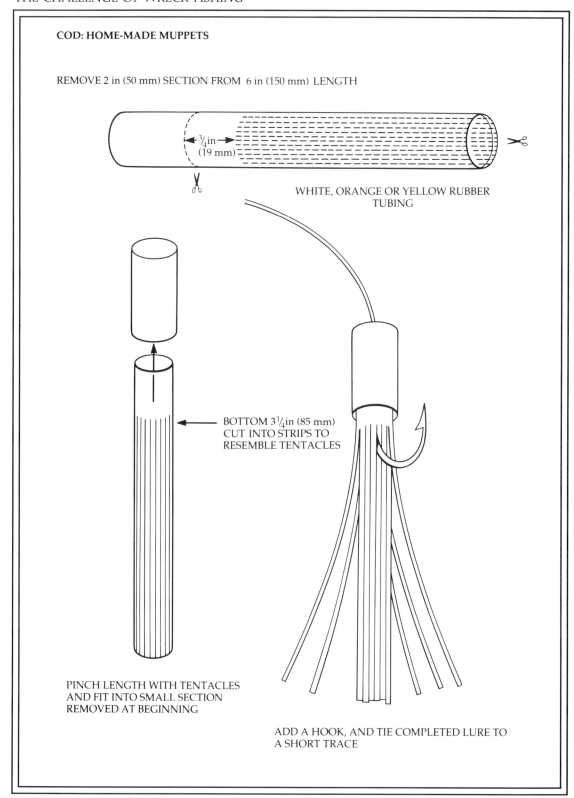

$\frac{3}{4}$in
(19 mm)

WHITE, ORANGE OR YELLOW RUBBER
TUBING

BOTTOM 3$\frac{1}{4}$in (85 mm)
CUT INTO STRIPS TO
RESEMBLE TENTACLES

PINCH LENGTH WITH TENTACLES
AND FIT INTO SMALL SECTION
REMOVED AT BEGINNING

ADD A HOOK, AND TIE COMPLETED LURE TO
A SHORT TRACE

than single-hook tackle. Just because you are using three hooks doesn't mean to say that you will get a cod on every one, so it may in fact pay you to experiment with a multi-rig. On the other hand, if you are going to use a pirk on its own, then you can get a lot of fun out of scaling down both your line and your tackle, perhaps using a multiplier loaded with 20 lb (9·1 kg) breaking strain line on an uptide boatcaster. You might not have the drawing power of several baits, but you will have an enjoyable scrap with every fish that you catch.

Multi-rigs can be used with either natural bait, muppets, feathers or artificial eels. I like to use muppets, cutting one strand of the dropper loop close to the main line so that there is plenty of trace to afford the lure as much movement as possible. This is not compulsory, but I find it helps. I tend to steer clear of artifical eels as I think their movement is too hampered by the pirks which I use at the bottom of the tackle, in this case the much larger home-made ones with the treble hook baited with a whole *calamari* squid. All in all, I think it is better to stick with the muppets off the droppers, as illustrated on page 70, but if I had no joy with these, then I would probably take off the muppets and replace them with either long, tapering strips of mackerel, or change the hooks to 6/0 Aberdeens and load them with as many lugworm as I could get on the trace. This method will often catch a decent cod, but it can get through a lot of bait and consequently be very expensive, unless, of course, you have dug your own.

If you experiment with single pirks, then there are a variety of ways in which you can increase your chances. One way is to add some smell by putting a natural bait on the treble. Formerly, another way was to get hold of some pirks, manufactured by Wilmek, which had a hollow compartment into which you could put some cottonwool impregnated with a scent additive. The body of the lure was drilled so that the smell could circulate in the water and act as an attractant. Unfortunately,

Wilmek went the way of so many small businesses and folded. Whether another company will take over the manufacture of these pirks still remains to be seen. If anyone does, then they should carefully examine the colour range which used to be on offer. This contained such colours as blue, which is probably the least efficient of all the colours for fishing, and some other shades which were almost as dubious. On the other hand, both the yellow and the chrome models were extremely effective.

Another way of increasing your chances is to add some sort of visual attractant. Cod are a very curious fish, often nosing around in the water and examining all sorts of bits of pieces. I remember one occasion when I saw a fish, in fairly shallow water, which appeared to be fascinated by a white, disposable teacup of the type used in vending machines. This had obviously suffered, being split in any number of places, but succeeded in holding the cod's attention for a couple of minutes. At the time, unfortunately, I had no fishing tackle on me, so I simply watched in interest. A few days after, while browsing through a local paper, I read that two small boys had jumped on a 20 lb (9·1 kg) cod as it swam close to the beach, then dragged it to the shore. There was even a photograph of the fish that they had mugged, its mouth open, I thought, in obvious surprise! Now I don't know whether it was the same fish, but in a seaside resort there is so much litter in the water that this particular individual may have had so much sensory input coming in that it had become distracted from the business of survival. A fatal mistake as it transpired. However, after pondering this for a while, I remembered a friend of mine who swore by the rather extreme tactic of putting seven or eight flounder spoons on the trace above his bait. Privately, I had dismissed that as overkill but, thinking about it afterwards, I wondered whether a much simpler, as in less bulky, compromise could be reached.

My first consideration was to ensure that any spoon was set up in such a way that it had

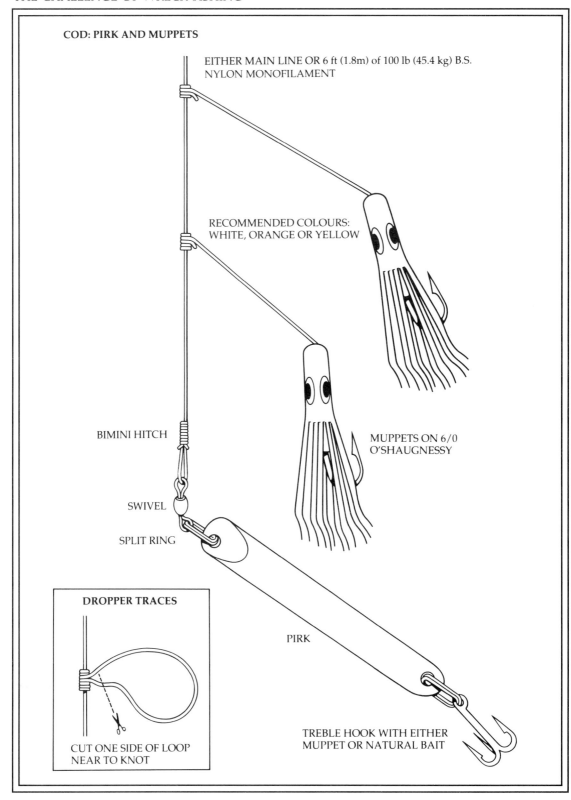

COD: PIRK AND MUPPETS

EITHER MAIN LINE OR 6 ft (1.8m) of 100 lb (45.4 kg) B.S.
NYLON MONOFILAMENT

RECOMMENDED COLOURS:
WHITE, ORANGE OR YELLOW

BIMINI HITCH

MUPPETS ON 6/0
O'SHAUGNESSY

SWIVEL

SPLIT RING

PIRK

DROPPER TRACES

CUT ONE SIDE OF LOOP
NEAR TO KNOT

TREBLE HOOK WITH EITHER
MUPPET OR NATURAL BAIT

complete freedom of rotation, especially if it was to be used above a pirk where the retrieve could give it a most attractive movement. A simple solution would be simply to attach it to one eye of a swivel by a split ring, then thread the other eye on to the main line between a couple of beads. This could then be secured in position by using either a bimini hitch to trap the beads or a telephone-wire stop. (These stops are made by taking a length of one of the fine inner wires of interior telephone cable, coiling it tightly about a nail, then sliding it off and cutting it into smaller pieces. One of these is then slid onto the line, held by one end and tightened by turning the coils between your thumb and forefinger. It then becomes longer and moulds itself to the diameter of the line, staying firmly in place unless moved either by the angler or by a reduction in the line's diameter, as happens when it is stretched.)

Watching this in the water, there seemed to be no particular problems, but neither was there quite the attraction which I had anticipated. It therefore occurred to me that, if I removed the third, central eye of a treble swivel, I could then pass the line through the hole that this left in the swivel's body, trap this between beads as usual, then connect not one, but two spoons, one to each remaining eye. In this way they were held apart and, more importantly, the revolutions about the main line were slowed, the final result of this being a simple, neat tackle that so far appears to be very effective and is very easy to construct. It is illustrated on page 72, shown in combination with natural bait.

When I use this tackle, I like to fish it from an uptide boatcaster such as the DAM Megalite Uptide CR, a budget-priced rod with an excellent action, which, because it is slightly longer than conventional boat-rods, gives very good control over any fish. It is also ideal for single-lure tackle for both pollack and cod. For reels, I tend to stick to such models as the Ryobi SLE 320, a level-wind that is excellent value for money, or the Shimano TR2000 LD Triton Charter Special, which is more expensive but combines both a level-wind and lever drag, the latter of which is far more user-friendly if you suddenly find yourself up against a bigger fish.

A last point, before leaving the subject of pirks, concerns the presentation of fillets of mackerel. If you are intending to use these as the natural bait, then you can make them look better by replacing the treble hook with a single 6/0 or even 8/0 Viking. Hook the flesh through just once, certainly no more than twice, and the fillet or strip can then flutter invitingly to add scent, taste and visual appeal.

Legering is the last method which I am going to examine, although not in any great detail as I refer to it in some depth in later chapters. Suffice to say that, whether or not you will be able to leger will depend, to a large extent, upon the strength of the current. This will not only determine the amount of lead necessary to hold the bottom, but will also strongly influence the skipper's decision as to whether or not to anchor up. Obviously, if he doesn't anchor, then it will not be possible to leger, although the tackle may be drifted with a fillet of mackerel or swiftly changed to a lure. If he does anchor up, and there is still a bit of current, then it may be a good idea to switch to a reel loaded with wire line, remembering, if you do, that at least the tip ring of the rod must be fitted with a roller. The advantage of this is that the current will have less effect upon the thinner diameter of wire line than it might upon a similar strength of nylon monofilament. The disadvantage is that kinks can form in the line if another angler gets his line wrapped around yours, causing a tangle which may need quite a lot of sorting out.

As far as the actual leger tackle for cod is concerned, it is not significantly different to the lure tackle used for pollack, except that the weight must be heavy enough to hold bottom and the lure should be replaced with either a whole *calamari* squid on a 4/0 to 6/0 O'Shaughnessy or several lugworm on a 6/0 Aberdeen. Both are effective baits but, if you

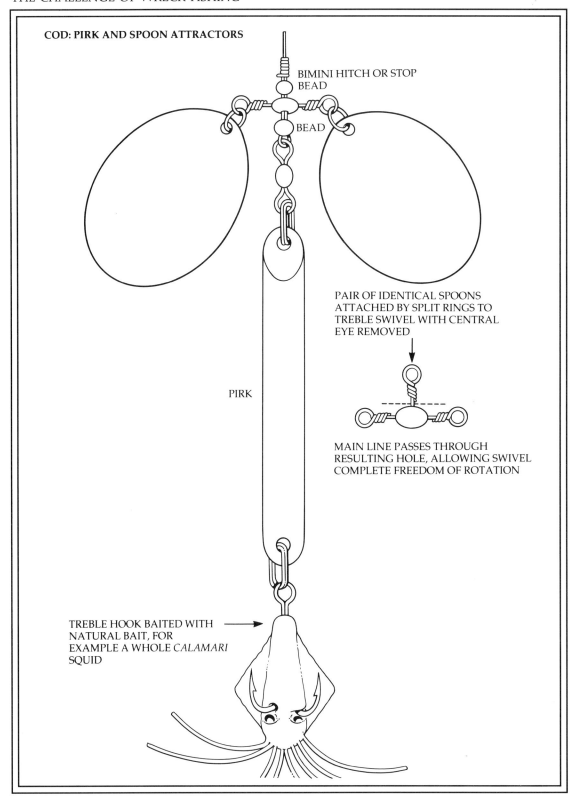

COD: PIRK AND SPOON ATTRACTORS

BIMINI HITCH OR STOP BEAD

BEAD

BEAD

PAIR OF IDENTICAL SPOONS ATTACHED BY SPLIT RINGS TO TREBLE SWIVEL WITH CENTRAL EYE REMOVED

PIRK

MAIN LINE PASSES THROUGH RESULTING HOLE, ALLOWING SWIVEL COMPLETE FREEDOM OF ROTATION

TREBLE HOOK BAITED WITH NATURAL BAIT, FOR EXAMPLE A WHOLE *CALAMARI* SQUID are intending to use lugworm, then you will find it will pay you to put a telephone-wire stop, then a free-sliding bead, about 12 in (300 mm) up from the hook. This will help to keep the bait together, but you may have a few problems with smaller fish, especially if the wreck holds large stocks of whiting or pout. This is not, perhaps, a nuisance if you like eating such fish and they are all of a good size, but it is sometimes annoying when you are sure that there are better fish to come aboard. If all you are getting is lots of small whiting, then take off the hook, replace it with a 4/0 O'Shaughnessy and tie on a size 6 Aberdeen on a 3 in (75 mm) trace to the bend of the larger hook. Put as many lugworm on this little trace as you can, then drop your tackle back down to the wreck. The result is a tackle which will catch a small fish and tether it to the spot. It is a useful tactic, especially when there are some biggies around, as a whiting secured in such a way, when a big cod is on the prowl, is really, if you will excuse the pun, in deep, deep trouble! And any cod, when he sucks in the smaller fish, will also suck in the larger hook, just as a carp sucks in a boilie. You wait for a second, make sure that he has it, then strike and set the hook. Then, far below, you will feel him nod as if he is acknowledging that the game is up. Don't be fooled, however, for it is just the beginning as you strive to bring him to the boat. If he is a biggie, it could be fun. If not — ah well, anyone fancy cod and chips?

CHAPTER SEVEN

CONGER EELS

The date was 4 November 1913. Eager eyes peered across the water to where the battleship, HMS *Empress of India*, gallantly stood by to perform one last, irrevocable service for its country, the ignoble fate reserved over the years for many ships whose tour of duty is finally over: gunnery practice. It was presumed that the ship would last for some time, protected as it was by a mild steel plating that was up to 17 in (430 mm) thick in places, but, unfortunately, its resistance was to be embarrassingly short. A shot from one of the smaller vessels set it on fire almost immediately; then, when the dreadnoughts opened up, it was holed below the waterline on one of the first salvoes, turned over and sank.

For a time the battleship was abandoned, a rusting hulk some 380 ft (116 m) long by 75ft (23 m) across the beam, until the first charter-boats discovered its position. Then, for a time, it produced some good catches of pollack, which, even now, it can occasionally repeat, but lying so close inshore it was inevitable that these stocks would be swiftly reduced until the charter-fleet lost interest and moved on, seeking new wrecks at ever-increasing distances from their home ports.

Fewer pollack swam over the ill-fated *Empress of India*, lying in her watery grave in some 150 ft (45 m) of water, but on her decks and in her hull there lurked some other, less obtrusive, denizens of the deep. Throughout the flood of the tide these hid in their lairs, but as the tide slackened they swarmed over the decks and round the wreck in their constant scavenging for food, giving divers a good chance to see just how large a population of conger eels the wreck had developed over the years.

Charter-boats returned from time to time, the large numbers of small eels giving good catches for their anglers, interspersed with the occasional bigger fish. Then, as numbers dwindled, fewer boats came to call upon the wreck, leaving her open to the advances of the specimen-seeker, the man prepared to wait for long periods in the hope of a monster eel.

For the wreck was not barren of conger. The earlier trips helped to clear away the smaller, faster fish, the younger conger eels that were inevitably first to the angler's bait, but behind them they left a core of larger, stronger fish that would test the angler's tackle and strength to the limits of their endurance. These eels, slower than the younger fish, travelled only short distances from their lairs, accepting bait and almost immediately backing into their hideaways with such determination and power that few were the anglers that could stop them.

Their bites were deceptive, a mild plucking that gave no indication of the size and ferocity of the fish beneath, but the angler, striking upwards, swiftly found himself straining to get the eel away from cover as quickly as he could, fighting his battle as far away from the wreck as possible. The conger, on the other hand, reacting to the sting of the hook, would strain just as hard to reach cover where, wrapping its tail around the wreck, it became inevitable that all the angler could do was pull for a break.

Different anglers tried different tactics, but most elected to use leger tackle with a very short, strong trace, either tied out of commercial monofilament, 120 lb (54·4 kg) breaking strain, possibly greater, or nylon-covered or single-strand wire. Long traces, which allowed the conger those extra few inches, enabling it to get a purchase upon the wreck, were usually discarded as they increased the chances of the conger but not the anglers.

Today, there are many inshore wrecks which, like the *Empress of India*, have been virtually abandoned by the charter-fleet and which are now the homes of some very large conger. That is not to say that you have to go to one to catch a big conger — you don't; many turn up even on virgin wrecks — but they do offer good specimen opportunities without the distraction of numbers of smaller fish. They also have the advantage of being closer to port, increasing the amount of actual fishing time over the wreck itself. It is a point which is worth bearing in mind.

If you are going to fish for conger, then the most important starting points are fresh bait and strong, reliable tackle. Congering is not a game of finesse, especially when you consider that a big eel can grow to over 100 lb (45·4 kg) with commercial reports of eels landed that are twice that size! They are a demanding species that will put a lot of strain on both you and your tackle, which must be man enough for the job. Frankly, I would not even think about using a rod of a class less than 50 lb (22·7 kg) rating. I would also like to see it equipped with roller rings throughout or, at the least, definitely the tip ring. If I thought there was a chance of a very big fish I might even step up to an 80 lb (36·3 kg) outfit.

If the rod has to be strong, then the reel simply has to match. You can forget about cheap alternatives here. If you are going to do any kind of serious congering then the reel has to have a very good clutch, with very smooth action, perhaps of the lever-drag type, and has to cope with the tremendous strain of getting

A conger has a vicious bite. Don't take any chances.

that eel away from cover as soon as you have hooked her. It also has to have a large spool which doesn't distort or buckle under pressure. That demands quality, which doesn't come cheaply. You might elect for a multiplier such as the Ryobi SLE 340, which is perfectly dependable and, at something over £100, one of the cheapest, most reliable reels around which still incorporates a level-wind, or a Shimano Triton with its precision engineering and silky-smooth drag. Alternatively, you could pay up to £300 plus for top-of-the-market models such as the Ryobi AD101SS — a power-assisted electric reel of tremendous strength and durability — or the Shimano Beastmasters which, although they are expensive, will give you long years of service and

Charles Armstrong aboard the Torquay-based charter-boat Striker *with his first-ever conger!*

are extremely unlikely ever to let you down.

I mentioned a level-wind because that is something I would not do without. I like to lock my hand fully around the rod without having to worry about guiding line onto a spool when it is taking me all my effort just to fight the fish on the other end of the rod. I also prefer level-winds for winding on wire line; they are much easier on the angler's thumb, particularly if the line is under any kind of pressure. The only problem is that there are nowhere near as many reels on the market with level-winds as there are reels without, which tends to limit your choice.

The most impressive level-wind multiplier that I tested was the Ryobi AD101SS Electric reel, which was lent to me primarily for the use of my friend Charles, who suffers from multiple sclerosis and is largely confined to a wheelchair. We had previously been out after conger but he had been unable, on conventional gear, to shift them from the bottom. Now the Ryobi needs a 12 volt power source, but on the occasion that he used it − in conjunction with a DAM Megalite IGFA CR 80 lb (36·3 kg) rod − which, incidentally, performed beautifully and also has the advantage of being very reasonably priced − the reel enabled him, after hooking an eel, to get it away from the wreck and play it out in midwater. At long last, after several trips which had been fruitless, we had finally put together tackle which allowed Charles both to hook and successfully to land a bigger fish.

If you ever get the chance to use one of these reels, then you will notice that the power facility is optional. You don't have to use it, but if you do then you can either set it to retrieve continuously or use your thumb and the option button to maintain complete control and discretion over the winding-in. You can still, if you prefer, wind in by hand, just like any other reel, but the power-wind does make it a lot easier and it is faster to boot. The only disadvantage is having to have a 12 volt battery handy, but as the reel is provided with about 3 yd (3 m) of cable, this does not represent a tremendous hardship and there are other advantages to compensate. For example, the rate of retrieve on power-wind is 90 yd (82 m) a minute and the drag, as you would expect, is very smooth and efficient. You can also change the position of the reel seat so that you can fish the reel beneath the rod if you happen to find this more comfortable. There are no problems with line-lay as the level-wind is very well engineered, although I don't recommend putting your thumb in its way to test how much pressure it can exert because I think that would be a very painful experience! Frankly, I think it is a superb reel and one for which I am saving my pennies at the moment.

Although there are some areas of fishing in which you can make economies very safely without losing any of the efficiency of the tackle, this does not, generally, apply to congering. Certainly there is no reason for you not to make your own traces and your own leads, but with the line, the rod and the reel you cannot afford to go for second best. If you do, you will lose fish. On the other hand, if you go for good-quality gear then your catch rate will reflect the improvement.

The line, whether wire, nylon or Dacron, undergoes a considerable amount of stress. Frankly, if it holds up for ten trips you are lucky. However, if you use the bimini hitch to tie both the main line and the wire trace − or heavy commercial monofilament if you prefer − then you will maximize the strength available. It is also not much use thinking that stronger line means you can put greater pressure upon the fish. It doesn't work that way. The most limiting factor is the amount of pressure that *you* can exert, that is, your own musculature. I once tried an experiment to see how much pressure an 80 lb (36·3 kg) outfit could transfer to the hook, but limited the main line to Ryobi 50 lb (22·7 kg) breaking strain Siglon Marine. The trace was 45 lb (20·4 kg) nylon-covered wire to a stainless steel 6/0 hook. At the end of a half-hour I had come to the conclusion that you would need to be superhuman to keep a steady pressure of even 30 lb (13·6 kg) upon the fish; 22 lb (10 kg) was much more likely to be the maximum that could be maintained, even then with considerable difficulty.

An interesting footnote was that, when two of us increased the pressure, pulling directly against the hook to see at what breaking strain the line would break, we were surprised by the hook itself snapping, an incident which has since been repeated upon a wreck trip. Neither the line nor the trace, both tied with biminis, showed the slightest inclination to part. However, when we replaced the bimini on the main line with a knot, then we found that the line would break, although usually at a pressure above that which a single angler could impose upon a struggling eel. Similarly, if we put crimps upon the trace, we found that these reduced the breaking strain to a fraction over half of its stated strength. In both cases, the bimini hitch was far more successful than conventional methods of tying tackle, completely obviating any need for lines above 50 lb (22·7 kg) breaking strain, the only exception being with heavy commercial monofilament for conger traces. This, of course, is subjected to a different type of stress; the eel will try to bite through the nylon and may even succeed if you are using nylon that is less than 120 lb (54·4 kg) breaking strain. It could not, however, bite through nylon-covered wire, enabling you to reduce the breaking strain to only 45 lb (20·4 kg)).

There are a few problems with tying bimini hitches in nylon-covered wire, but these can be overcome by tying one end of the trace roughly to a large swivel, perhaps hanging freely on a cup hook that is firmly screwed into position. All you do then is to slide a good swivel, perhaps a 1/0 stainless Berkley swivel onto the trace, let it slide to the stop on the bimini-hitch tool and tie the hitch so that the swivel hangs freely on the loop. As you make the hitch, pulling firmly against the swivel hanging on the cup hook, you should occasionally relax the pressure just enough for the swivel to rotate and allow the wire line to

free itself of any potential kinks. Once you have tied the proper swivel on, simply hang this over the cup hook, cut the other swivel from the trace, then repeat the procedure with the hook. The finished result is very neat, particularly if you pull the finishing knots tight with judicious pressure from a pair of pliers, and strong enough to cope with even the biggest of eels.

The leger tackle I use is illustrated opposite. It is essentially very simple, with the wire trace to the hook attached by a sturdy split link to a second wire trace, which itself connects to the swivel on the end of the main line — which is also hanging freely on a bimini hitch. The plastic tubing on the reel line sheaths the hitch and prevents tangles while the weight simply hangs from an Ajusti slider, zip slider or similar. I don't use spoons, attractors, etc. near the hook as I have found that congers generally dislike anything moving about near the bait.

However, just because you cannot use a visual attractor, doesn't mean to say that you cannot use a scent attractor. One idea that I liked (see page 80) was to make up some boat leads, using a fairly long eye made out of galvanized wire. I squeezed this fairly closely together so that I could slide on a swimfeeder, then opened the end and twisted it with a screwdriver, at the same time enlarging the eye so that the swimfeeder could not possibly fall off. When you use one of these leads you can either fill the swimfeeder full of cotton-wool and then inject it with a scent additive, for example, pilchard oil, or simply fill it with the entrails of the mackerel which you are using for bait. Either method will set up a strong scent trail to enhance the effectiveness of your tackle.

Scent is important, which is why you must use the freshest bait that you can get hold of — or the smelliest, like *calamari* squid which does, however, seem to take more ling than conger. If you are going to use mackerel, then a whole side of one that has just been caught is a very good bait. Simply pass the hook through the

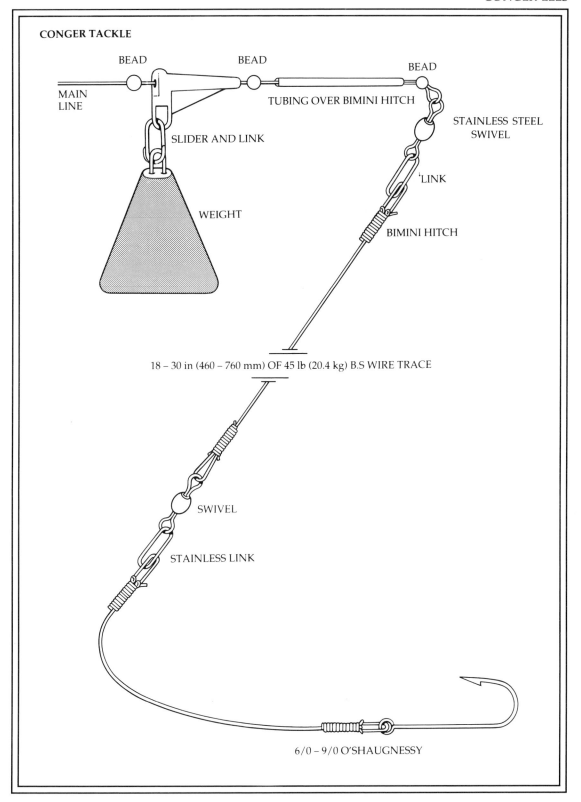

CONGER TACKLE

BEAD

BEAD

BEAD

MAIN LINE

TUBING OVER BIMINI HITCH

STAINLESS STEEL SWIVEL

SLIDER AND LINK

'LINK

WEIGHT

BIMINI HITCH

18 – 30 in (460 – 760 mm) OF 45 lb (20.4 kg) B.S WIRE TRACE

SWIVEL

STAINLESS LINK

6/0 – 9/0 O'SHAUGNESSY

CONGER: SWIMFEEDER AND WEIGHT

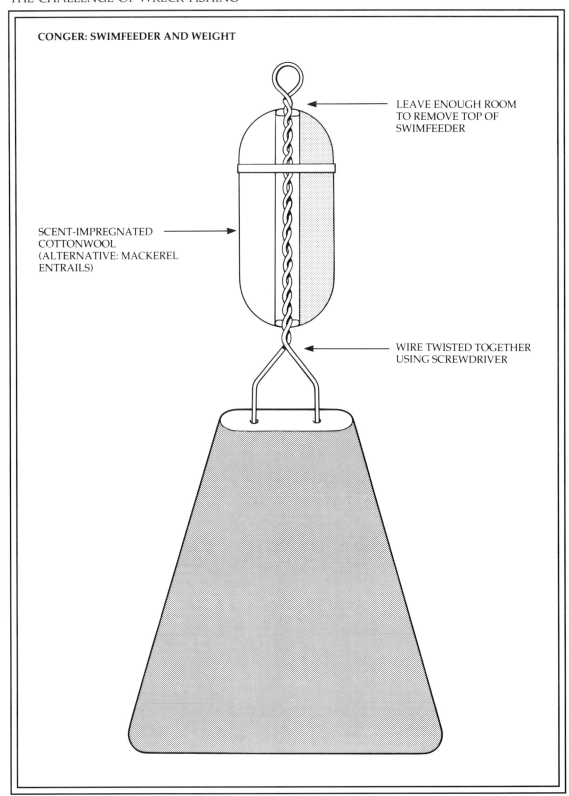

LEAVE ENOUGH ROOM
TO REMOVE TOP OF
SWIMFEEDER

SCENT-IMPREGNATED
COTTONWOOL
(ALTERNATIVE: MACKEREL
ENTRAILS)

WIRE TWISTED TOGETHER
USING SCREWDRIVER

tail end, turn it and pass it twice more through the flesh, working up towards the opposite end. You can also make use of the head, hooking it once through the eye sockets. This has taken a number of fish over the years although it does seem to be more effective if you leave as much of the entrails trailing as possible.

Conger are not shy of a big bait. I have known one large one caught on a 5 lb (2·26 kg) pollack deadbait, although this is an extreme to which I personally would not go. However, every bait should be as fresh as possible. Conger dislike frozen bait, something which divers have discovered in congers which they have hand-fed over the years. So, if you are stuck in the position of having to use frozen bait, then stick it in a bucket of water and make sure that it is well thawed by the time you get to the wreck. It may not be fresh, but at least it will not be cold and completely unattractive to the fish.

When your bait finally tempts a conger, you might be surprised by the gentleness with which they can take it. Don't be fooled, however. That gentleness lasts only until it feels the hook – which should be both large and strong, perhaps a 6/0 or even an 8/0 Viking or O'Shaughnessy. At that point, the conger will make a determined bid for cover, which you must stop if you are to have any chance at all of landing the fish. You have to get it up and away from the wreck, placing the power of your muscles directly against the power of the eel. It is a brutal contest of strength, for you are not fighting the weight of the fish, you are fighting its muscular development, just as the fish is fighting yours.

A big eel will tax not only yourself, but every item of your tackle, especially the swivels as it spins through the water, or indeed out of it after the gaff has gone home. They have to be up to the job. One thing you will find, however, is that the tackle shown (page 79) has definite advantages of speed in getting your tackle back down to the bottom. All you have to do is unclip the trace and put on a new

A conger taken close inshore.

one. Time enough to recover the old when the eel is dead (gutted and beheaded). One thing you really want to avoid is messing around trying to get your hook out of a large and very angry eel, which, quite frankly, is either asking for the hook to be transferred to your hand or risking a few fingers. More than once I have seen anglers with their thumbs impaled on a hook, all from trying to get the hook out of a fish too early in the day. If the skipper wants to try it, then that is up to him, but I don't recommend that you do.

If you are only catching small eels, which you might not want to keep, then very often the skipper will have a tool made for unhooking and releasing the eel. This is a good idea as the conger is one of the few species which can survive the pressure changes of being brought up from the depths to the surface. Once returned, it can grow bigger and eventually get its crack at breeding, a migration which it is thought to make only once in its lifetime and which ultimately ends in its demise.

Curious really, if you think about it, that a 100 lb (45 kg) eel, or indeed almost any eel over approximately 12 lb (5·4 kg) is going to be a sexually immature female.

CHAPTER EIGHT

LING

While you are fishing for conger, you may be surprised by the capture of a ling, a member of the cod family that looks a bit like a cross between a cod and a conger. It has a barbule on the chin and an extended body that ends with a powerful tail quite separate from the dorsal and anal fins. Coloration is brown with a pale underneath, while the anal fin starts well back towards the tail. Size obviously varies with the individual, but ling can grow to a substantial weight, with specimens in excess of 60 lb (27·2 kg) occasionally reported by commercial fishermen.

As its powerful jaws and barbule suggest, the ling is a predator that does most of its feeding either on or just off the bottom. It fights well, certainly in the early stages, and is obliging to anglers in that it has a decided appetite for mackerel and *calamari* squid and can be tempted by a variety of methods. Basically, the tackle used for eels will occasionally tempt the odd ling, but for greater numbers you will probably find it helpful to put on a longer trace. Ling will also feed with a bit of current running, so it is not unusual to catch the most both before and after the time during which congers are feeding.

If you are going to use bottom tackle, then you can often minimize tackle losses by placing a float upon the trace in much the same way as you might rig a buoyant leger for flounder from the shore (see page 84). The main difference is that the float is much larger and may be fished in conjunction with pennel rig, essentially a small hook baited with rag-worm or similar and tied to the bend of the larger hook which you intend for the bigger fish. The idea is that a small fish is attracted by the wormbait, takes it and is then tethered to the larger hook in the same way as a carp angler fishes a boilie from a hair rig. When a predator then takes the smaller fish, it is often hooked much nearer the mouth than is usually the case, enabling you to unhook it both easily and with the minimum of distress to the fish. However, having said that, ling cannot endure changes in pressure as well as conger. It is kinder to boat the fish, kill it and unhook it in that order, particularly as the swim-bladder will often have erupted into its mouth.

The advantage of the pennel rig is that you should, with a bit of luck, have caught one of the smaller fish upon which the ling are already feeding. The float then helps to keep it in plain sight until the attention of a predator is attracted. Your bait is absolutely fresh and in keeping with the natural food supply upon the wreck. One thing you might have to watch is getting bothered with wrasse, which are not such a good bait. In that case, try baiting the smaller hook with a tiny sliver of mackerel, which is far less likely to attract the unwelcome attentions of either ballan or cuckoo wrasse, the principal two species found on most wrecks.

You don't have to use a pennel; instead try using a single large hook, perhaps a 6/0 O'Shaughnessy baited with mackerel strip. The current will lift the float — and the bait — into plain sight and give the strip at least the

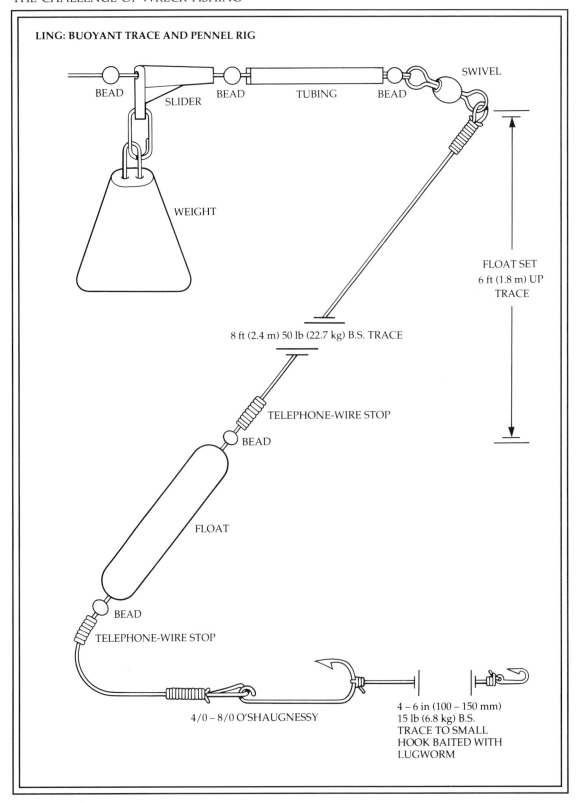

LING: BUOYANT TRACE AND PENNEL RIG

BEAD

SLIDER

BEAD

TUBING

BEAD

SWIVEL

WEIGHT

FLOAT SET
6 ft (1.8 m) UP
TRACE

8 ft (2.4 m) 50 lb (22.7 kg) B.S. TRACE

TELEPHONE-WIRE STOP

BEAD

FLOAT

BEAD

TELEPHONE-WIRE STOP

4/0 – 8/0 O'SHAUGNESSY

4 – 6 in (100 – 150 mm)
15 lb (6.8 kg) B.S.
TRACE TO SMALL
HOOK BAITED WITH
LUGWORM

John Ripley holds up a large ling caught on a fillet of fresh mackerel.

semblance of motion, which is very attractive to ling. Results are still pretty good, probably better in terms of numbers, but not as good in respect of the size of the ling that you catch.

A popular method of fishing for ling is to fish a pirk with a couple of muppets tied paternoster-style above it. The pirk itself has a muppet covering the shank of the treble hook, although a useful alternative is to place a swivel directly onto the split ring to the pirk, then an oval link to both the swivel and the treble hook. Instead of using a muppet you can then cut a small hole in the top of a *calamari* squid, remove the swivel etc. from the pirk and mount the deadbait, then re-connect the swivel to the pirk. In this way you are presenting both sight and smell to the ling.

When I have tried this method I have found that it outfished pirks which were equipped with yellow and black muppets, which, in turn, outfished pirks equipped with muppets of different colours and which then, in their turn, outfished plain pirks. However, another useful tactic was to take a plain pirk and simply hang a sizeable strip of mackerel over each point of the treble hook. This was then proved to be just as successful as using a *calamari* squid, although the strips didn't last anywhere near as long as the squid.

From time to time I have fished a combination leger and pirk rig, which is set up almost exactly as the conger rig in Chapter 7. The only difference is that the trace is a 6–8 ft (1·8–2·4 m) length of 120 lb (54·4 kg) breaking strain nylon monofilament and that the weight is provided by a pirk which hangs on the Ajusti slider in the same way as the lead would otherwise have done (see diagram opposite). The tubing acts as an anti-tangle rig and the results have been quite acceptable. I have started by working the pirk, but then, if bites have been shy, paused to let the trace run out in the tide. I usually found that I could then connect with any fish that had missed the pirk on its first attempt.

The only thing which I did find was that the tackle was most successful if the pirk had been

mounted with a *calamari* deadbait in the way described. It also took the occasional conger and sometimes a pollack upon the retrieve. On the longer trace, I usually baited the hook with a half-fillet of mackerel, cut lengthways to make a long and tempting strip of flesh.

Ling bites can be deceptive, sometimes being hard but often being no more than a couple of determined plucks. Strike quickly and try to get the fish up and away from the bottom, then let the fish expend itself in midwater. The fight is good at the beginning, but the fish will usually be unable to cope with the pressure changes as it nears the surface. Once you have it beaten, get it up and kill it humanely.

Ling are quite nice to eat, with flesh that is both firm and tasty, some people rating it higher than cod. A big ling, however, can provide a lot of meals, even if you freeze it down for future consumption. After you have caught a few, why not have a go at catching something different? You already have your meals, so why not change the pirk for a lighter weight and the trace with a single hook for a longer trace with a plug on it. You will still catch the occasional ling, but you will also find yourself bringing aboard bass, if you are lucky, or the occasional pollack.

Generally, although ling do grow to a large size, you can fish for them with much lighter tackle than you would use for conger. I usually use a 30 lb (13·6 kg) class outfit, matched with a lever-drag level-wind, or an uptide boatcasting rod, matched with a similar multiplier. I find that the uptide rod gives me extra leverage, but can be awkward to slip into the butt pad which I habitually wear, the length of the handle to the reel seat making it an uncomfortable stretch for the arms. To counter this, some companies, such as Conoflex, have released blanks which have an inbuilt reducer; in these a piece of carbon or fibreglass actually retracts within the blank itself, but they can be extended to give a better spacing for casting. However, you don't need to cast for wrecking, so whether you want to try the lighter

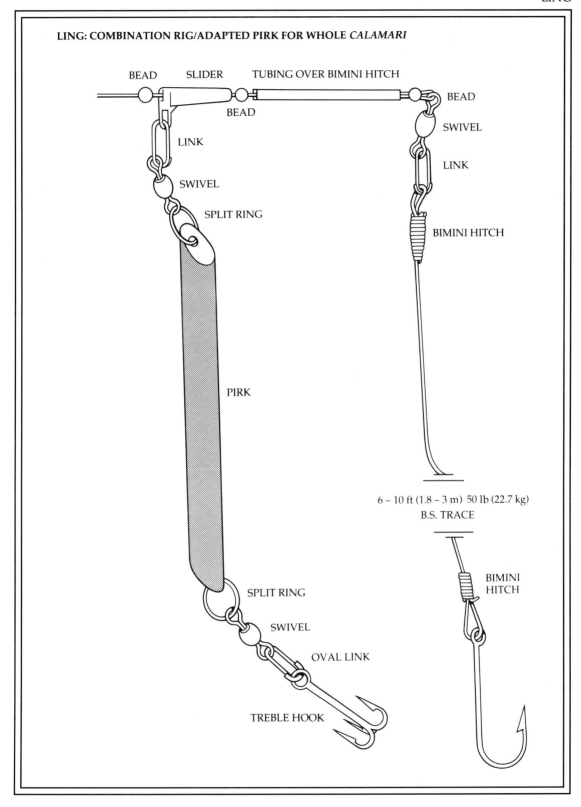

LING: COMBINATION RIG/ADAPTED PIRK FOR WHOLE *CALAMARI*

BEAD   SLIDER   TUBING OVER BIMINI HITCH

BEAD

BEAD

SWIVEL

LINK

LINK

SWIVEL

SPLIT RING

BIMINI HITCH

PIRK

6 – 10 ft (1.8 – 3 m) 50 lb (22.7 kg)
B.S. TRACE

SPLIT RING

SWIVEL

BIMINI
HITCH

OVAL LINK

TREBLE HOOK

COMBINATION MUPPET AND BAITED SPOON

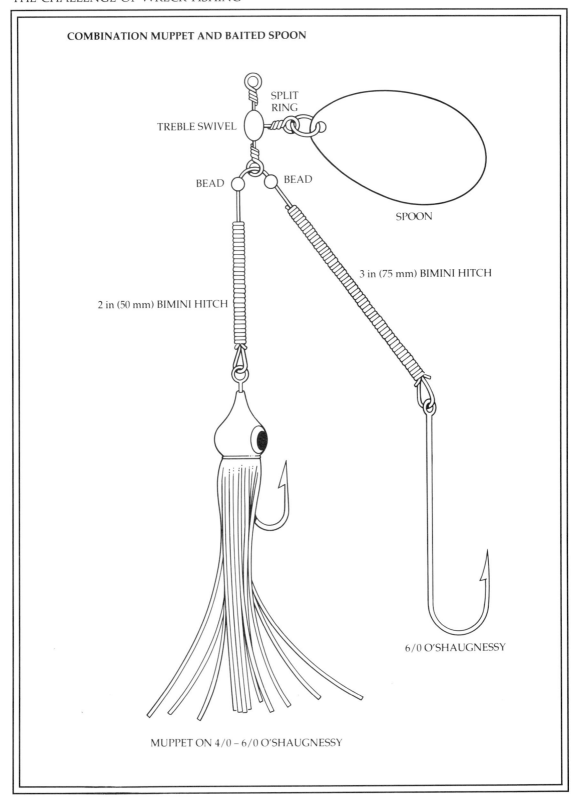

SPLIT RING

TREBLE SWIVEL

SPOON

BEAD   BEAD

3 in (75 mm) BIMINI HITCH

2 in (50 mm) BIMINI HITCH

6/0 O'SHAUGNESSY

MUPPET ON 4/0 – 6/0 O'SHAUGNESSY

uptiders or just stick to conventional rods is entirely up to you. Both will catch fish.

Another method of going for ling is to fish for them in the same way as for pollack, with flying-collar rig. This is a very sporting method, but bites are few and far between, almost invariably on large yellow or large black rubber eels. However, if you stick with the largest of say, black Redgills or Eddystones, you will also find yourself catching a fair number of pollack. A combination which I would like to see come out would be an $11\frac{1}{4}$ in (285 mm) Eddystone with the back black and the sides and belly fluorescent yellow. Similarly, an $8\frac{1}{4}$ in (210mm) Redgill with mackerel-striping in yellow and black might be very effective, especially in wrecks which lie in deeper water.

Instead of using a rubber eel, you might experiment with Roland Martin spinner baits, especially those where the skirt on the hook closely resembles a yellow muppet, albeit the tentacles are finer. These have accounted for some very good catches, but seem equally effective for pollack and coalfish. In order to make the tackle a bit more discriminatory towards ling, I experimented with some heavy-gauge monofilament and ended up with a rather strange-looking arrangement that was a combination of a baited spoon, a treble swivel and a muppet. However, the tackle boasted two hooks instead of one and was much more stepped up towards sea-fishing and wrecking in particular.

The diagram opposite should make the tackle clear, but I must point out that it depends on the bimini hitch for success, because the 'arms' of the tackle are so stiff that they act in almost the same way as a metal boom. The treble swivel is also important as the third eye allows the spoon to rotate above both the muppet and the bait in a very attractive manner. Now you could, if you wanted, make the tackle out of stainless-steel wire, but it would not have the flexibility that the nylon allows. However, it would be quite easy to make if you wanted to experiment in that direction. As for the spoon, you might cut the handle from a metal dessert spoon and adapt it to your purposes, or you might choose to experiment with flounder spoons or a whole range of other attractors. Whatever you decide, I think that the tackle has considerable potential, but it will be interesting to compare notes once it becomes more widely used. In the meantime, I hope that you do decide to experiment and wish you every success with your attempts. Angling, contrary to the way in which many people choose to portray it, does not stand still. Tackle changes and so does our knowledge of fish. There is no such thing as a 'perfect' rig for any species, but there are methods which show a degree of success. What you can do is to take any information that is offered and adapt it to your own, individual fishing style. At the end of the day it is what you catch that is important, not what other people might think. People sometimes laugh at my tackles, almost always at the beginning of a trip. They are not usually laughing at the end and that, I think, is quite important.

CHAPTER NINE

THE OCCASIONAL SHARK

My first encounter with a shark came shortly after I had purchased my first-ever boat, a small inflatable that came with a 4 hp motor, but which was so light that I ended up launching it from all manner of unlikely places. Further, because there was so little weight to it, I soon found that it had a good turn of speed, nipping out to marks which, if I had had a particle of common sense, should have been the last places on my mind. As it was, I travelled blithely onwards, sometimes miles out to sea, often passing some of the larger boats with their heavier, traditional hulls. It was a time of great excitement and exploration, when I could search out marks and places that I had only dreamed of visiting before! This excitement, I might add, was heightened by the fragility of the air-filled tubes that lay between myself and the depths which I could only guess at and wonder.

I suppose, given these circumstances, that it was only natural to search for some wrecks close to shore, particularly when the rumour reached me of two wrecks, possibly lying quite close together, which were within easy reach of even so small a craft as I possessed.

No-one seemed to know their exact position but, by listening to different people and the comments of divers, I decided to fish a particular mark which seemed just as likely as any other to be the spot where the two ships went down. Consequently, on one beautiful day, I untied the boat from the roof-rack of my car, tucked in my tackle and slipped into the freshness of the early morning, gliding over a

sea so calm that it seemed more like tinted glass than water. There was not a breath of wind and I soon found myself floating in what I had been assured was some 80 ft (24 m) of water, quietly dropping my tackle over the side and watching it disappear, the tail of the lure frantically waving as it chased the weight out of sight.

Seven or eight times I drifted some 300 to 400 yd (about 0·3 km), each time hoping to come into contact with some of the pollack that divers reported. Unfortunately, on each occasion there was nothing, no sign of any interest in the lure that I was using. Then, because I was in an area which was noted for its mackerel, I decided to catch a few for bait, to see if this would improve both my chances and my dwindling morale. I reached for my lighter rod, then turned in surprise as a shoal seemed to materialize at the side of the boat, racing through the water with a speed that made me instantly suspect the presence of bass. Quickly I turned to reach for the rod set up with a lure, then stopped, suddenly deeply apprehensive, as a sliding, scraping noise seemed to come from beneath the wooden floor. The inflatable rocked, then a great blue-grey head appeared at the front of the boat, seemed to nonchalantly dismiss both myself and my craft as unworthy of further note, then slowly, after what seemed an age but was probably only seconds, turned to cruise leisurely in the direction which the shoal had taken.

Looking back, this first shark was probably only a baby porbeagle, trying to scrape off some of the parasites that occasionally adhere to the dorsal fins, but, I have to admit, at the time, I had quite a different view, no sooner watching this performance than wishing myself at quite some distance from that particular spot. It made me apprehensive, but from that apprehension grew the resolve that I would get to know and to understand the British sharks, their habits, how to tell them apart, how dangerous they were — and the way in which you could catch them on rod and line.

Consequently, I went first to the local library and, from there, to speak to skippers, to anglers and even to the newspapers and divers. As I began to become further involved with the subject, I quickly learned that anglers' knowledge, although it served repeatedly to pull aboard blue sharks, porbeagles, threshers, even the occasional mako, was by no means as comprehensive as they thought. For a start, these four species, having dominated catches for years, were by no means the only visitors to British waters. Hammerheads, apparently ranging in size from a few feet to as many as 20 ft (6 m) in length, had occasionally been seen, one grizzled old seaman even recalling a day in 1963 when a pair cruised leisurely around the end of Paignton pier, perhaps only 50 yd (48 m) from bathers in the shallows. Other sharks, identity unknown, but also ranging in length to over 20 ft (6 m), had occasionally appeared and even harried anglers' baits as they sought to bring aboard the fish that they caught over wrecks. The further south I researched, the more numerous such reports became, until it became obvious that there are, from time to time, some very big sharks in British waters; these, however, do not belong to any of the four well-known species and have yet to be caught and clearly identified. It also became obvious, as more and more boats began to explore waters much further afield, that some of those boats, while operating in waters closer to France than to Britain, were having such encounters more often in prolonged spells of hot weather than

at any other time. In short, the information which I was gathering seem to indicate that, as the water temperature rose, bigger sharks were tempted from further afield to enter and explore British waters.

To date, those big shark, with the exception of the instantly recognizable hammerheads, have still to be identified. However, as sightings of hammerheads seem once again to be on the increase, so one begins to wonder how long it will be before one of these spectacular fighters will appear upon the British record list. I remember a day, probably in 1989, reading a newspaper in which I came across an article stating that there had been over 100 sightings of hammerheads in Cornish waters. Now if that were true, and not simply newspaper hype, then the chances of an angler connecting with one of those fish must be increasing in proportion to the increased number of fish. It has not happened yet, or if it has then the angler has not landed it, but I think, as we see the water temperature rising in line with the greenhouse effect, that the day will come.

Realistically, there is another explanation: the anglers I spoke to were possibly unfamiliar with sharks native to Britain and exaggerated the proportions of any that they saw, perhaps even confusing their features as soon as the shark was out of sight. However, it boggles the imagination to think of any person confusing, say, a blue with a hammerhead, sightings of which are most often reported during spells of hot, sunny weather. Certainly, with native British species, there does seem to be a much better chance of landing fish in prolonged warm conditions than in unsettled, colder spells when the water temperature drops. Most of the captures made are reported in the few months from July to September, when the water temperature is nearing its peak, and it is on this period that the serious shark-angler will concentrate his attention.

You may wonder what this has to do with wrecks, but their unique set of conditions offers shark a hunting ground which is rich in both variety and quantity of prey. This means that many wrecks will be visited by shark and, in taking steps to be prepared for just such a chance encounter, the dedicated wreck-angler seems likely, sooner or later, to find himself with a unique opportunity to catch what may be the biggest fish that he or she will ever encounter. If you are ready, you could be in with the chance of catching that fish of a lifetime. If you are not, then you might find yourself bitterly regretting such a wasted opportunity.

Take, for example, blue shark. As the most common British shark these turn up on wrecks fairly regularly, sometimes taking up a position beneath a charter-boat and helping themselves to any fish which the anglers are desperately trying to get on board. If this happens, then the only way to discourage the shark, whose appetite will otherwise both stagger and appall you, is to adopt some retaliatory measures, offering him one fish too many, so to speak, with this final gift bearing a very large hook and mounted on 250 lb (113·4 kg) breaking strain wire, made up as shown in the diagram opposite. Don't bother with the bimini hitch for this breaking strain of wire, as it would be almost impossible to tie, and quite unnecessary in any case. The thickness of the wire is for no other reason than to combat the powerful jaws of the shark, as there is not the remotest chance of breaking such a trace, even if crimps have reduced its breaking strain by 50 per cent. You could not put that much pressure through a rod, no matter how hard you tried.

I wish I could tell you of a glorious fight should the shark decide to take your bait. Unfortunately, the blue tends to make one very long run, then turns and makes only half-hearted attempts after that. Any struggle is soon over, with more losses made through the angler's clumsiness than from any determination on the part of the shark.

Once you have caught him, however, the experience should at least deter him from taking any more of the fish that you are pulling

up. If it doesn't, then move to another wreck.

If this last statement puzzles you, then I should make clear that I would like to see the shark put back alive in the water, indeed never removed from it at all. If you use the quick-release rig illustrated on page 94, you can simply cut the wire at the point shown and allow the shark to swim free. It will soon get rid of the hook on its own, so you need not fear that leaving it in will cause any irreparable damage. After all, you have to be realistic. Unless the shark was hooked in the outside of the mouth, it would be unwise in the extreme to try and unhook it, at least while it was alive. As for killing it, well, quite frankly, over the years, so many anglers have done just that, posing beside their trophies for the inevitable photographs, that the blue, like others, has suffered a serious diminution of numbers. A few years ago, when the photographs shown here were taken, no-one particularly worried about keeping the fish for a photograph. Nowadays, stocks have suffered so much that every one kept puts in further jeopardy the species' prospects for survival. And, let us face it, so long as you have caught it, what does it matter if you let it go? You can always identify it and the skipper will be able to give you a pretty reasonable estimate of its weight. As for a photograph, take your camera with you. That way you will have a permanent record while the shark is released to grow bigger, breed and live to fight again.

Identifying blues is not really a problem, as they have several distinctive features. The most telling are the slim body, long, pointed and curved pectoral fins and the comparatively small gill slits. The first dorsal fin, nearest the head, is larger than the second, but both are relatively small. If you particularly want to look in the mouth, then you might also notice that the teeth are triangular with a serrated cutting edge. As for its colour, well, as you might expect, this tends to be dark blue above, becoming lighter on the sides and white on the belly.

Most people who try for blues will, as the

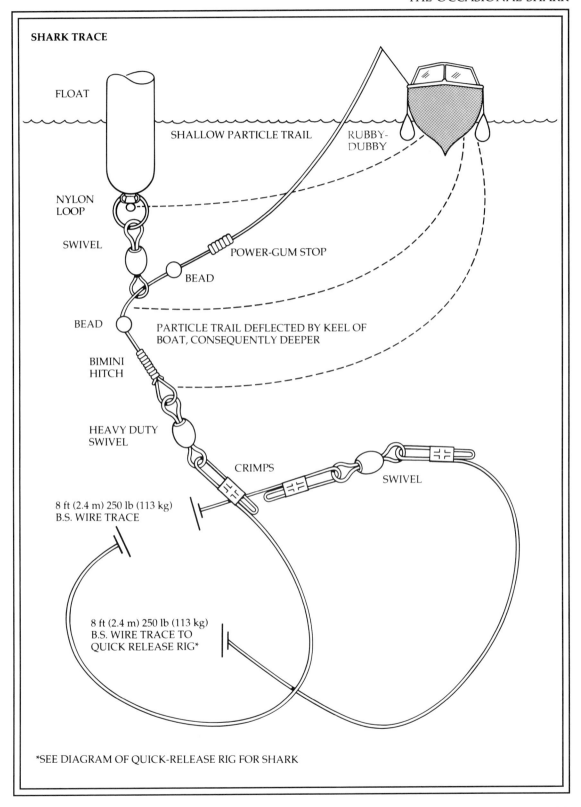

SHARK TRACE

FLOAT

SHALLOW PARTICLE TRAIL

RUBBY-DUBBY

NYLON LOOP

SWIVEL

POWER-GUM STOP

BEAD

BEAD

PARTICLE TRAIL DEFLECTED BY KEEL OF BOAT, CONSEQUENTLY DEEPER

BIMINI HITCH

HEAVY DUTY SWIVEL

CRIMPS

SWIVEL

8 ft (2.4 m) 250 lb (113 kg) B.S. WIRE TRACE

8 ft (2.4 m) 250 lb (113 kg) B.S. WIRE TRACE TO QUICK RELEASE RIG*

*SEE DIAGRAM OF QUICK-RELEASE RIG FOR SHARK

SHARK: QUICK-RELEASE RIG

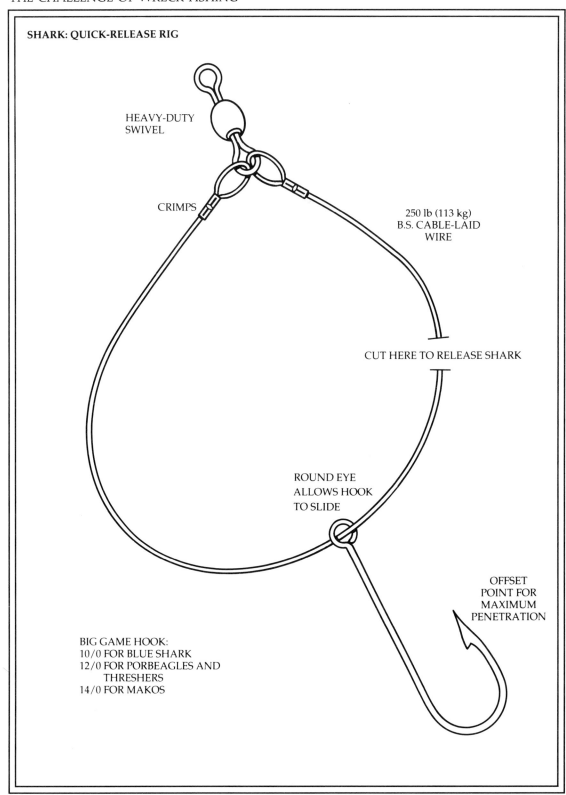

HEAVY-DUTY
SWIVEL

CRIMPS

250 lb (113 kg)
B.S. CABLE-LAID
WIRE

CUT HERE TO RELEASE SHARK

ROUND EYE
ALLOWS HOOK
TO SLIDE

OFFSET
POINT FOR
MAXIMUM
PENETRATION

BIG GAME HOOK:
10/0 FOR BLUE SHARK
12/0 FOR PORBEAGLES AND
    THRESHERS
14/0 FOR MAKOS

HOME-MADE SHARK FLOAT

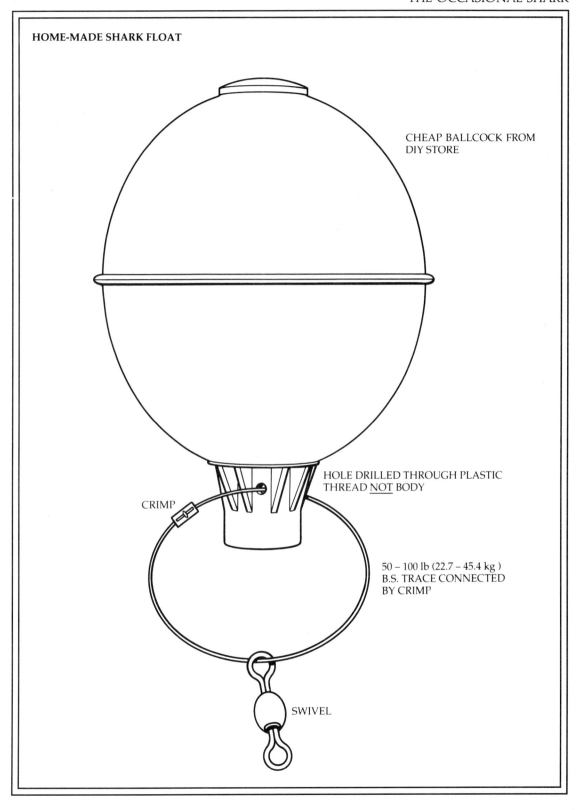

CHEAP BALLCOCK FROM
DIY STORE

HOLE DRILLED THROUGH PLASTIC
THREAD <u>NOT</u> BODY

CRIMP

50 – 100 lb (22.7 – 45.4 kg)
B.S. TRACE CONNECTED
BY CRIMP

SWIVEL

diagram on page 93 suggests, use both floats and rubby-dubby. Now as far as floats are concerned all you need is something to hold up the weight of the trace and a big bait. There are a variety of things you can use, but the ones that I prefer are simply made out of plastic ballcocks. These can be picked up very cheaply, costing less new than a conventional float for shore fishing if you shop around, but they are neat, easily adapted and highly visible. Some people use detergent bottles, others balloons; still others use pop bottles or other disposable containers. My only comment is that, while balloons work, they can sometimes attract the attention of seagulls. The end result is a punctured balloon and annoyance to the angler. I have yet to meet a gull that could puncture a ballcock! As for its adaptation, all you need do is to drill a small hole through the screw thread at the bottom, then pass through some nylon monofilament, slide on a swivel and crimp the two ends together so that it makes a loop with the swivel free-sliding upon it. When you tackle up, you put on your main line a bead, the other eye of the swivel and another bead, then tie on a swivel which will connect to the trace by a split or oval link. The depth is then determined by a power-gum stop which is tied to your main line as shown in the diagrams on the right.

This kind of stop is neat enough not to jam in the tip ring, but is soft enough to slide up or down to adjust the depth at which you are fishing. Some companies make little plastic clips which you screw to the line at an appropriate point, because they believe that this is simpler, but I really don't like having to unscrew such a device from the main line at the moment when a very angry shark is getting close to the boat. If he makes a sudden lunge then the angler can be taken unawares and everything is lost! It doesn't seem a very god idea to me, especially not when the line is also being jammed between hard plastic edges, with the possibility that it may be damaged in the process. The quick-release rig

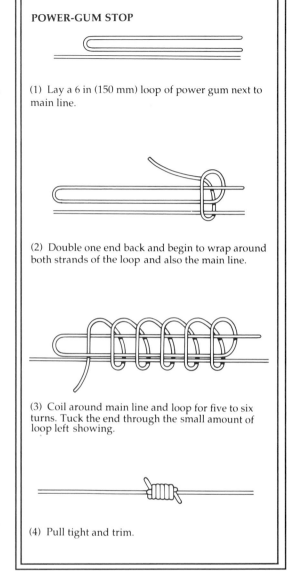

POWER-GUM STOP

(1) Lay a 6 in (150 mm) loop of power gum next to main line.

(2) Double one end back and begin to wrap around both strands of the loop and also the main line.

(3) Coil around main line and loop for five to six turns. Tuck the end through the small amount of loop left showing.

(4) Pull tight and trim.

has already been described (page 92; illustrated on page 94) but I will spend a moment talking about hooks. Sharks, despite their reputation for ferocity, can be finicky in their handling of your bait. They will often reject it if something happens to alert their suspicions. From this point of view, it is better to use a hook with a round eye, this eye being of sufficient size to slide freely on the loop of the quick-release rig. When a shark mouths the bait, the hook moves and adds no resistance to make it suspicious. The shark may then gently move off, while you should be standing up, pointing the tip of your rod down and towards the fish, thumbing the spool which is running freely for the release of line. After a few moments, the shark will usually stop, turn the bait and swallow, then move off a second time, which is when you strike upwards while locking the spool. At this crucial moment you will find that an offset point will penetrate much more effectively than a straight one, requiring far less effort and giving a much better hold.

The fight you get will then depend on the species that you have hooked. Porbeagles, unlike blues, which are by far the tamest of British sharks, fight long and hard, making determined dives and occasionally killing themselves in the process. Makos don't seem to know when to stop and threshers can be nearly as determined as porbeagles and far more acrobatic in their attempts to escape.

One thing you have to bear in mind, no matter what species you have hooked, is that it helps to stay mobile, moving from one side of the boat to the other so as to be always in the best position for keeping in contact with the fish. It will also be easier if you have a good skipper to rely on, for in a determined fight there is little possibility of the boat simply holding station while you play the fish out. For example, if the shark runs toward the boat, the skipper will often circle towards the shark, bringing the boat about so that he can follow in the shark's path. This can be tricky, particularly as many shark will try to scrape the line beneath the keel of the boat. If a shark succeeds in doing this, then the chances are that the line will break and the shark will escape. If it doesn't, then you may find only a temporary respite as the shark doubles back to try it again. You must stop it from succeeding, because even if the line doesn't break the first time, it will not be able to stand up to much more of that kind of rough treatment. To do this, you have to be on your toes, anticipating

what the fish will do and placing yourself in the best position to frustrate its design. This means using your head as well as your muscles, not simply expecting the skipper to do everything for you. If you beat the fish, and you should, then it will be through both of your efforts. If you don't, well, the experience will at least have been valuable, a sort of dress rehearsal for the next time when you do beat the fish.

One thing all shark have in common is an excellent sense of smell, a trait which anglers appeal to when they make up rubby-dubby bags. Essentially, a rubby-dubby is a mesh bag containing lots of chopped-up fish, entrails, pilchard oil and whatever other attractors the angler thinks may draw the fish to the boat. If he can see the shark, then he will hang the bag on the side of the boat from which he is fishing. This will then begin to lay up a scent trail very close to the surface, attracting and encouraging sharks to feed at shallow depths. If, however, the angler suspects that any shark are running deep, then he will put the rubby-dubby on the opposite side of the boat, where the resulting scent trail will be deflected deeper by the keel. In both cases, this use of groundbait has been repeatedly shown to be highly effective, but it does get through a considerable number of mackerel.

All British species can be fished for in the same way, using the same tackle but with the variation suggested in the size of hooks. However, both porbeagles and blues have also been caught on large freshwater plugs, particularly the big red-and-white ones which are so popular in the USA and Canada. Now these plugs are *big*! By which I mean some 14 in (355 mm) in length. They are also very expensive and rely on the fish being close to the surface, where the angler can judge their response to the lure, for example, by casting to it, trolling slowly past, working it, etc. It is a method which has not caught on significantly, but it does work and can be very exciting to watch. It may not have the aerial acrobatics of American tactics for taking hammerhead sharks (where the angler, literally, flies a kite with a whole-mullet bait hitting the surface of the water until a big hammerhead throws itself after the bait in a spectacular fashion) but there is considerable tension in the 'will it, won't it' moment as a shark draws close to the lure.

I have not heard of a mako or thresher hitting a plug, but will go into some detail about their appearance so that, whatever method you use, you should be able to identify accurately the species which you have caught. However, before I deal with these somewhat rarer sharks, I think it would be a good idea to become familiar with the characteristics of the porbeagle. This is a much sturdier-built shark than the blue, with gill slits that are very much larger. It has pointed teeth for seizing and holding prey, while the first dorsal fin is large and starts just behind the pectoral fins. The second dorsal is very small and positioned directly above the anal fin, which is also small. There is a small 'keel' set just below the middle of the tail and a lateral 'keel' along either side of the tail column. Coloration tends to bluish-grey, sometimes brown on the back, while the belly is white. Those that are found in our waters run to a larger size than the comparatively small blues that we catch: a porbeagle of 465 lb (210·9 kg) has been recorded whereas a 218 lb (98·9 kg) blue dominated the record list for years.

Threshers are immediately identifiable by their extremely long, curved tail. The gill slits are only moderate in size while the teeth are small, triangular and with a smooth cutting edge. Their pectoral fins (the ones on the side) are very large, while the second dorsal and anal fins are by contrast very small. The first dorsal is large. The fish's body coloration tends towards grey, black or blue-grey above, becoming lighter underneath. As far as size goes they grow to 1,000 lb (453·6 kg) in weight, but those caught on rod and line tend to weigh under 300 lb (136 kg).

Makos are the least often reported of the sharks around our coast, although what they lack in numbers they make up for in ferocity

and size; the British record, at the time of writing, stands at 500 lb (226·8 kg). They also live almost exclusively in the upper 65 ft (20 m), which is why comparatively shallow baits seem to be the most frequently successful. As for appearance, the mako is a slim-bodied shark, usually either deep blue or blue-grey above while the underneath is white. The snout is pointed and the teeth are long and slender with those on the lower jaw set forward of the lip. The gill slits are large, as is the first dorsal fin, while the second dorsal is very small and set over and slightly forward of the equally small anal fin.

Whichever species you try to catch, you will often find that you can tempt them with a variety of baits. Fresh mackerel is widely used and successful, but garfish, though not often used, can also be deadly. Small baitfish, such as fresh sprats, small pout, etc., are easily available although you have to make them more appealing by using several fish on the hook instead of one. A good method of doing this is to hook several in a bunch, passing the point through their eye sockets so they hang in a uniform manner on the shank. Basically, your bait must be big enough to attract the shark in the first place. If all you can get are tiny mackerel, then rig two of them together so that they at least provide enough bulk to be interesting. Herring are another good bait, but for these to be successful they need to be as fresh and as appealing as possible. Again, if the fish are small, then put enough on the hook to make the shark want to take it. The end product may bear no resemblance to a living, swimming fish, but if it has plenty of scent, releases blood and is big enough to fool a shark into thinking it is an easy meal, then you can still be confident because it has a lot to make it attractive.

You should also take care over your selection of tackle. Simply because shark are big is no reason to fish for them with the angling equivalent of derricks! If you are careful, then you can fish for them with a comparatively-light outfit. You might, for example, fish for blues with 20 lb or 30 lb (9·1 kg or 13·6 kg) class tackle matched to an appropriate breaking strain of line and a wire trace some 12 ft (3·7 m) in length. For porbeagles or threshers, you might step up to 30–50 lb (13·6–22·7 kg) tackle, again with 12 ft (3·7 m) of wire trace and the strength of your main line matched to the rod that you are using. As for makos, despite their fearsome reputation, you really don't need to exceed an 80 lb (36·3 kg) rod and could even scale down to a 50 lb (22·7 kg) outfit. The only thing I would suggest, however, is that you increase the length of your wire trace to at least 18 ft (5·5 m). That way, if a mako gets frisky near the boat, then the 250 lb (113·4 kg) breaking strain wire will take a lot of punishment which your main line simply could not cope with. Shorten the trace and all you will find is that you are drastically reducing your chances.

Incidentally, an important safety tip. Never grip the wire with your bare hand and never wrap the trace around it. If you do, and the shark makes a sudden lunge, then you could find yourself with a truly horrific injury. That is why it is so important, when you get that far, not to try and bring the shark too quickly to the boat. Make sure that it is properly played out. The last thing you want is to lose it at the last minute because you tried to bully it before it was really ready for the final stages of the fight.

All in all, British shark-fishing, like so many other fields of angling, is a question of common sense and preparation. Now that preparation, at least for wreck-anglers, might only take the form of an hour spent in making up tackles just in case one appears. However, if it does, then that hour may prove to be one of the most productive that you have ever spent. On the other hand, if you simply dismiss the possibilities of shark, then you may find yourself wishing that you had put at least a couple of traces in your bag. You may even find yourself severely disappointed that you didn't have a plastic ballcock! It is a case of contingency planning, but when that contingency is so greatly to be desired, then surely it is a shame to be caught unprepared and unawares. If you are, well, that is the way it goes. If you are not, ah, then you can send in your photograph to the local paper, preferably one that shows the fish in the water as you prepare to let it go.

And, of course, so long as you have not forgotten your camera...

CHAPTER TEN

THE OLD AND THE NEW

In this chapter I am going to examine some of the species which are taken over wrecks, but which, for one reason or another, tend to be slightly overlooked in the pre occupation with the fish mentioned so far. Some of them are fairly familiar, like the red and black breams, turbot and rays, while others, like the wrasse, are neglected because anglers prefer to fish for things which they can eat. Another reason, I think, is that people don't realize the size to which some of these wrasse can grow. Perhaps, if it was more commonly known that there are fish to dwarf the British record on any number of wrecks, then it might be a different story. As it is, most of the wrasse caught are taken by accident, as are bass, spurdogs, smooth-hound, John Dories and any number of oddities that occasionally turn up. Together, these represent the unexplored potential of many wrecks, a potential which this chapter can only begin to reveal. If you turn your own ingenuity in this direction, then you may be surprised to find that a wreck-trip may satisfy not only traditional expectations, but may also be a passport to an undersea realm, where the citizens are many and varied and, perhaps, not quite as predictable as you expected.

Within these pages I can offer some help, some introductions, section by section, to a few of their number. However, one of the most exciting things about wreck-fishing is that there is never any hard-and-fast guarantee as to exactly what you are going to catch. Frankly, if you are prepared to experiment,

then you could find yourself in the position of never knowing what you have caught until it finally appears in those telling few feet between the keel of the boat and the surface. You will also find that the rewards implicit within such an approach include not only the greater range of fish to be caught, but also the satisfaction and excitement which will fill you every time you catch a new species, colouring the trip with a pleasure which will linger in memory long after the boat has finally returned to port.

However, for now, let us once again return to that undersea realm, where I will introduce you to the first of its citizens, our namesake, the angler-fish.

ANGLER-FISH

The first things which you notice about an angler-fish are the long stalks and the hanging flap of flesh which protrude above its great cavern of a mouth. These comprise the lure which the angler-fish uses to attract fish to within striking range, waving it subtly to and fro until a curious fish, drawn irresistibly to the siren promise of food, suddenly finds itself trapped as the angler-fish launches upwards with bewildering speed. The prey has little time in which to escape and, as the hunter has usually judged both distance and reactions to a nicety, very little chance of doing so.

With its quarry eaten, the angler-fish resumes its position, waving that deadly rod with such instinctive skill that once again it draws prey to within its range. Then, with the brown, mottled colours of its body blending in with its background, it manages to camouflage itself until that fatal moment when the smaller fish has reached the point of no return. It is an effective, if somewhat brutal, means of ambush, and a variety of species are trapped, ranging from whiting and pout, as you might expect, to gurnards, dogfish, pollack and even, in shallow water, the occasional cormorant.

So what does this tell us as anglers? To start with it is obvious that the fish themselves are slow-moving; that is why they wait for prey to come to them instead of chasing it in the manner of faster fish like the bass. It also tells us that it is accustomed to its food — most probably small fish, squid or cuttlefish — coming down from above. Lastly, it tells us that it eats live prey as opposed to feeding off carrion.

To make the best use of this information, we can approach the problem of catching it in one of two ways. The first is to set up a buoyant pennel rig in the way described in Chapter 8 for ling. This has the advantage of catching the natural and expected food upon which the angler-fish hunts. It then tethers whatever takes the bait to a position fairly close to the seabed, or very close if you shorten the trace to no more than 3 ft (about 1 m). The bait is then visible and secured within easy reach of predators. If an angler-fish comes along, and there is a good chance that one will, for although they are not common, they are certainly more plentiful than many people think, then that smaller fish stands a very good chance of attracting it for you to catch.

The second method, not quite as likely to succeed, but still offering a good chance, is to fish a long, flowing leger on the sandbank at the side of the wreck. The hook is baited with a *calamari* squid, or a small fish such as a sprat, which then is either inflated with air from a hypodermic syringe or has a float trapped somewhere in its body. The current streams the bait away from the weight, which must be heavy enough to firmly hold the bottom, and

gives it at least some appearance of, if not life, at least of being only recently dead. This may tempt a fish to take, especially if that fish has become used to feeding on the remnants of congers' meals as they drift with the current away from the wreck.

An extra advantage that you will find with these methods is that they will, from time to time, tempt other species, especially cod if sprat shoals are in evidence on the wreck. This makes for more interesting fishing, increasing the quantity if not the variety of your possible catch. However, if you are lucky enough to catch an angler-fish, don't be put off by its repulsive appearance. They are very good eating, with sections from the tail occasionally served up as mock scampi on even the most discerning of tables.

In fact, it could be argued that the only disappointing thing about angler-fish is their lack of fight. The last one that I caught resembled nothing more closely than a weed-covered rock in its steady drag from the bottom to the surface. The only time I received any clue that it might be alive was when it started swimming straight upwards, making my line go slack as it overtook it on the way up. Still, it is nice to catch one, both for its novelty and eating value, especially if it is one of the really big ones weighing around the 80 lb (36·3 kg) mark which, although thin on the ground, have occasionally been taken. I have not yet connected with one of these giants, but I keep telling myself that it is only a question of time. It will happen one day. I hope!

BASS

The majority of anglers are already familiar with bass through both shore-angling and inshore boat fishing. To them this silvery-grey fish, with its spiny dorsal fin, razor-sharp gill slits and deep, powerful body, is a worthy protagonist whose capture is especially valued. However, as far as wreck fishing is concerned, the number of people who actually try for them is very limited. It is not that their prestige has diminished; it is simply that people don't tend to equate the bass with captures made over wrecks. They just don't expect them to be there and consequently don't usually spare them a second thought.

For this, and other reasons, it may surprise a number of those people to discover that bass, far from being absent, actually flock to wrecks during certain weeks of the year, feeding heavily upon the ample stocks of smaller fish as they travel along their migratory paths. At this time they can be present in considerable numbers, which include many whose weight reaches into double figures. A few come into contact with anglers' baits, as you might expect, but these are usually almost accidental captures, the baits having been intended for other species. However, enough of these accidents have occurred to make some skippers suspicious, with the result that they have subsequently made and compared notes concerning the wrecks in their region. The next stage was inevitable, with some very good catches recorded by anglers who suspected their presence and tried to catch them deliberately.

I wish I could now say that such and such a month and state of tide was the time to go for these fish. Unfortunately, I cannot, purely and simply because there seems to be little similarity between regions. In some areas this influx appears to take place in late April/early May, possibly while the fish are *en route* to the marks that they frequent in anticipation of the peeler-crab bonanza in June. In other regions it appears to be much later, although still in the summer months. The best advice I can give is to discuss with your intended skipper whether he remembers any particular month as showing a few bass on the wrecks. If he can, then that will be the time to try.

As far as methods are concerned, the most successful captures reported to me were made by anglers who used lure tackle made up as for pollack, but with either fluorescent-orange Redgills or plugs of assorted colours substituted for the artificial eel. Both of these

methods were successful, but it became speedily apparent that the orange Redgills would also take pollack, often in very good numbers, as you might expect, and that the most successful plugs were various of the Rapala models, including the Original and the Slivers. Large plugs took more fish than small ones.

Other successful methods included legering with a long flowing trace to a size 2/0 Aberdeen baited with live sand-eel (this method also took the occasional turbot and then doubled up for pollack if the angler retrieved his tackle slowly each time that he wanted to check that his bait was still in order) and paternoster tackle baited with peeler crab. I suspect that other methods will emerge as time goes by, but for the moment these seem to be the ones to concentrate upon, especially as each of them is attractive to more species than just the bass.

BREAM

The most common bream which are found in British wrecks, in season, are red bream and black bream. The red bream is a fairly deep-bodied fish with the suggestion of a Y-shaped tail. Its eyes are very large and the dorsal fin is spiny. The pectoral fins are long and sickle-shaped, rising upwards when laid flat against the body and extending beyond the beginning of the anal fin. Its colour is (surprise! surprise!) red, but it may sometimes appear to have lengthwise streaks, an optical effect produced by the arrangement of the scales. There is also a conspicuous black mark set forward and above the pectoral fins, in the immediate vicinity of the start of the lateral line.

The black bream may be immediately distinguished from the red by the colour which, despite its name, is inclined more towards a blue or purple-grey above and silvery-grey on the sides, with a hint of either a gold or metallic sheen. Young black bream may occasionally show a tendency towards pink-coloured sides, and this has sometimes led people into mistaking them for red bream. If you get one like this, then look at the pectoral fins, which are smaller than in the red bream, and also for the mark behind the shoulder. If there is no mark, the fish is definitely not a red bream. Dark, vertical bands of colour suggest a male black bream, while the body shape of the black bream is somewhat more compressed than the red.

Other species occasionally turn up, of which the largest is commonly known as the dentex or the four-toothed sparus. It is infrequently captured and so is not really worth devoting a lot of time to. However, should you catch, as once happened in Dingle Bay, a 28 lb (12·7 kg) bream which looks like a red but has no dark patch on the shoulder, then you will know that you have connected with one of these fish. Other characteristics are occasional dark spots on the upper flanks and, sometimes, the head appears to have a hump set over and slightly forward of the eyes.

Gilthead bream have been taken from a variety of marks in recent years, most often from the south and south-west of England. They can be distinguished from the other species of bream by their unusual and striking coloration. This can tend towards grey, blue, red or purple above, with green on the head, silvery sides and a golden band between the eyes (hence the name). Other characteristics are dark spots at the base of the pectoral fins and the fact that its eyes are smaller than in the red bream. There is also a dark patch of colour near the gill covers.

One of the most enjoyable things about breaming is that you can scale down to using very light tackle, from spinning rods some 8 ft (2·4 m) in length to a 9 ft (2·74 m) baitcaster with a trigger-grip multiplier handle. The latter is much used in Canadian waters for spinning for small and large-mouthed bass, but has yet to make any real impact over here, which is a great pity. There was some experimentation with it, particularly a couple of years ago, but this was overshadowed by the impact of carp rods for shore-fishing. In the ensuing rush of publicity for the carp rods, the shorter baitcasters, which are superb for light

boatwork, were overlooked and almost forgotten. However, one day, both manufacturers and the public may realize that these baitcasters, matched with a suitable small multiplier, are one of the most forgiving and pleasurable outfits that it is possible to use. They are brilliant for both shore and boat, casting long distances with spinners and float tackle where required, or tackling such boat species as bream with an action that makes the very best of the fight. If you go on an inland holiday, they will even double superbly for spinning for pike, which ultimately renders them one of the most versatile outfits which it is possible to buy, or at least would be if people realized just how good they were and the manufacturers made them more commonly available!

You would probably enjoy using such a rod, if you could only get hold of one, perhaps even one of the discontinued Ryobi Masterpikes. If you can't, then an alternative is the Ryobi Wanderer/Stalking/Lure rod, a 9 ft (2·74 m) model which doesn't have a trigger grip, but which can still be used successfully with light multipliers. You may feel a bit nervous at first, its 2 lb (0·9 kg) test curve seeming very light for over wrecks, but when you consider that a Nile perch of 127 lb (57·6 kg) was taken on this rod, then that should at least give you some idea of its capabilities. You might also have a look at some of the heavier spinning rods supplied by other tackle manufacturers, especially the 9-footers (2·74 m rods) designed with pike in mind. These tend to have a better tip action and are useful should you come into contact with a bigger fish.

Whichever model you buy, you should ensure that you match it with an appropriate reel. One of the best that I know is the Ryobi T2, which has the innovative feature of being an ambidextrous multiplier. It is a gift for left-handed anglers and is combined with a 4·7 gear ratio which makes them ideal for breaming. The line capacity, which is 260 yd (238 m) of 14 lb (6·4 kg) breaking strain, is also ideal. If a pollack suddenly takes your bait, then you have a very good chance of bringing it aboard, the sensitive drag system allowing you to play the fish out in midwater, which, broadly speaking, is an advantage common to most multipliers. This makes them far more suitable for light boat-work than fixed spools which, on a personal level, I would not even consider using.

Another reel worth looking at is the Silstar Nova 20, a useful little reel which comes at an affordable price for those on a tight budget. It is an excellent reel for use in combination with a trigger grip. ABU also offers several other models which are worth looking at, even if they do cost a bit more, while Daiwa Millionaires are affordable and offer very good value for money.

You can, if you like, use an uptide boatcaster. If your budget is stretched, then it is probably sensible to get one of these because of the range of species which you can aim for. Unfortunately, compared with a baitcaster, they make for extremely dull handling of bream. They will have no trouble with bigger fish, but as far as bream are concerned it is a bit like using a sledgehammer to crack a nut, unless, of course, you intend to catch more than one fish at a time.

If such is your intention, then you will find that a paternoster-style of rig, as illustrated opposite, is ideal for your requirements. This is simple to make and easy to use, the swivels not being prone to the twisting of the line which can cause so many problems with booms. In the illustration two hooks only are shown which, on the lighter outfit, is the maximum that I would use with either a 12 lb (5·4 kg) or, at the most, 15 lb (6·8 kg) breaking strain line. If you were going to use an uptider, then you could safely increase the number of hooks to three and up the breaking strain of your main line to 20 lb (9·1 kg). This is not overly sporting, but it will catch fish, bearing in mind that the greater the diameter of your line, the greater the amount of lead needed to hold you in the right position.

An enjoyable alternative, given a lighter outfit, is to use a form of leger which allows the bait to stream out with the tide. Essentially this is the same as the lure tackle illustrated in Chapter 5, but with all of its proportions scaled down to allow the bream a sporting chance. The line, for example, might be only 10 lb (4·5 kg) breaking strain with either a 6 lb or 8 lb (2·7 kg or 3·6 kg) breaking strain trace. The Ajusti slider will have been replaced with a much smaller carp bead and the weight may be as light as 2–3 oz (57–85 g), depending on the current.

To use this tackle correctly, you should start by dropping down to the bottom. Your weight, if it is the right size, will slowly lift, enabling you to let out a little line and work it further away from the boat. Now a bream may take at any time, but, once you have succeeded in putting a reasonable distance between you and your tackle, you may often induce one to take by starting to retrieve line at a steady pace. If one does, then you will have a really good fight with the lighter outfit, but you will also have a pretty good idea as to exactly where the fish are, so the next time you go down you can get your bait fairly quickly to the area where you last found the shoal.

Please bear in mind, however, that this method of working the tackle is very different to just dropping down and letting the line out. All that achieves is a very large bow which can get right under the boat and cause all sorts of problems with anglers fishing the other side. If you think about it, the stern is going to be the best place to try out this method, preferably when the boat has settled to anchor. Once it has settled, you will find that the boat has swung round with the bow facing into the tide and your bait, once lowered from the stern, will be gradually drifted downtide without causing any inconvenience to other anglers.

You also need to consider timing. I have already mentioned that bream are a seasonal fish, but the extent of that season will depend on the part of the coast which you are fishing.

BREAM: PATERNOSTER

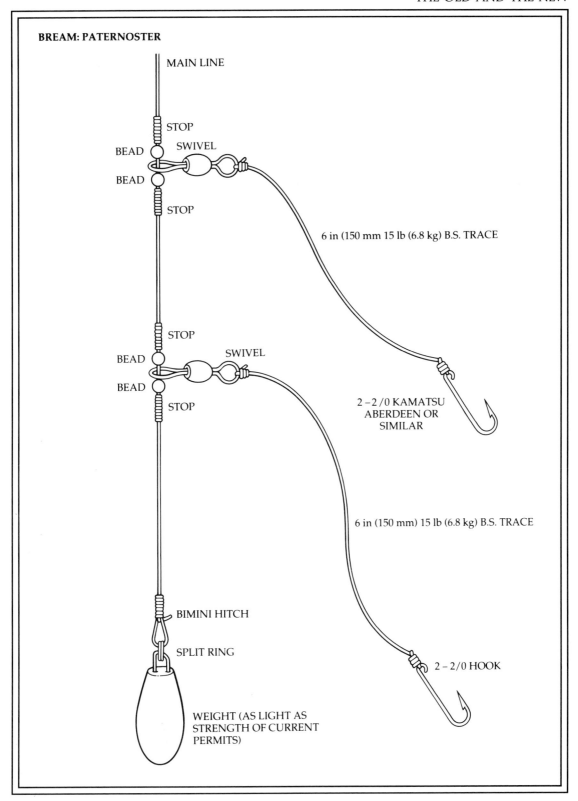

MAIN LINE

STOP

BEAD

SWIVEL

BEAD

STOP

6 in (150 mm 15 lb (6.8 kg) B.S. TRACE

STOP

BEAD

SWIVEL

BEAD

STOP

2 – 2/0 KAMATSU
ABERDEEN OR
SIMILAR

6 in (150 mm) 15 lb (6.8 kg) B.S. TRACE

BIMINI HITCH

SPLIT RING

2 – 2/0 HOOK

WEIGHT (AS LIGHT AS
STRENGTH OF CURRENT
PERMITS)

For example, one boatman in Dorset swore by a 6-week season while the fish continued to migrate in a south-westerly direction. His season started in April, sometimes continuing through to June, while the more southerly ports experienced their main runs at varying times between the middle of May and the beginning of September, at which point the fish then reversed their seasonal migration, presumably travelling back in the direction from which they came. Frankly, your skipper is the best person to ask, especially if he has been in business for quite some time as he will have built up experience of his marks over several seasons. With this knowledge, he should have a pretty good idea as to how they are likely to fish.

He is also worth quizzing on the subject of bait. Small strips of mackerel bait are almost universally successful, albeit to differing degrees, but nearly every port has found that a particular bait may at times be more successful than others. Some swear by cocktail baits, perhaps lugworm tipped with mackerel or squid strip, while others swear by lugworm and mussel. Still others prefer slipper limpet and squid strip. To a large extent, if you think about it, the successful baits must be determined by the type of food supply which the fish are encountering. If a particular item is plentiful, then the fish may become pre-occupied with it to the exclusion of everything else. Then, as their migration takes them to regions where perhaps another bait becomes the primary food source, so their attention will be diverted to whatever this new item may be. What we have to do is to anticipate what they are likely to find, then plan our ambush accordingly.

If you catch a bream, you will soon discover that they make very good eating, besides being a very sporting fish. Unfortunately, their migration, proceeding by a well-identified route, makes them vulnerable to commercial depredation. However, if you are willing to try for them, especially on longer trips which take you closer to France, then an experienced skipper will usually be able to put you amongst fish. The rest is up to you.

DOGFISH

Four types of dogfish are commonly found over wrecks: lesser and greater spotted dogfish, smooth-hounds and spur-dogs. The first species is of comparatively little sporting value, being so easy to catch from both shore and inshore boat that it seems a waste of time and money to try for them over wrecks. It is a small, voracious bottom-feeder that is more likely to bite on its tail as it is brought to the surface than to put up a decent scrap. Unfortunately, as it has an acute sense of smell, it can sometimes be awkward to avoid it if you are trying for other species. Over the years I have taken quite a number, most of them weighing less than 2 lb (0·9 kg), which have swallowed a whole *calamari* squid intended for bigger and better fish. However, if you do want to catch them, then just put down a simple leger with the whole head of a *calamari* on a size 2/0 Aberdeen. Make your trace about 6 ft (1·8 m) in length and strike upon the bite.

When you get them aboard, you have to be careful as to how you handle them, for they have a skin which is just as abrasive as sandpaper and which can give the unwary a very nasty graze. The best thing to do is to immobilize the head against the tail, holding both in the same hand, then whip the hook out as quickly as possible. Being an Aberdeen, this will straighten if the fish is too securely hooked, so you can get it out without having to resort to a pair of pliers. After that you can either let it go or keep it for skinning and eating.

Leger tackle that is baited in this manner will not only take lesser spotted dogfish, but also whiting, pout, the occasional pollack, turbot, rays, gurnard and bull huss (another name for the greater spotted dogfish). However, if you are trying for the latter, then it might be just as well to make your trace out of wire and bait it with a long sliver of mackerel, which they seem to prefer. As for the wire,

A lesser spotted dogfish. Sometimes these are present in such numbers that it is difficult to get through to better fish.

that is only there in case you find yourself suddenly tussling with a conger, not on account of any frenzied determination on the part of the bull huss to escape, which is, unfortunately, not very likely. In fact, the only thing that makes these more interesting than their smaller cousins is the fact that they grow to a greater size, specimens in excess of 20 lb (9·1 kg) having been occasionally recorded.

Both types of dogfish are similar in appearance, although the greater spotted can be recognized by the fact that its nasal flaps are lobed and its anal fin ends roughly halfway beneath the second dorsal. Its coloration also tends towards brown or russet-brown with large, dark patches of colour instead of small, round spots. However, both species are fairly slim-bodied with two small dorsal fins set on the back half of the body, starting just behind the pelvic fins. The underneath appears to be slightly flattened and is white in the case of the lesser spotted dogfish, which is also a much lighter brown on top than its heavier relation.

Smooth-hound, although associated with dogfish, are actually members of the tope family, albeit not as gracefully designed as their bigger relations. Their fins are fairly large, and the first dorsal is set further forward than is usually the case in members of the shark family. Gill slits are small and the teeth are flattened and designed for crushing rather than tearing, a feature shared with the rays. Coloration tends towards grey above and white on the belly, with some pale spots on the back and sides.

As the teeth might suggest, smooth-hound exist by feeding heavily upon crustaceans and spend most of their lives scouring the bottom for hard-backed crabs, hermit crabs and the like. They are much better fighters than either of the spotted dogfish and they grow large enough to be interesting. Unfortunately, there is little information regarding their presence near wrecks, although divers have reported seeing them in fair numbers. It is interesting to note, however, that trawlers seldom seem to catch them, at least in comparison with other species, which might indicate that they haunt the types of ground where trawlers are unwilling to risk their nets. If that is the case, then the ground close to wrecks should offer a good opportunity to catch a really big one.

Tackle should again be fairly simple, perhaps a leger with a wire trace to a hard-backed swimming crab or a de-shelled hermit. The wire is necessary because this type of bait may also attract a big wrasse, whose teeth would make very short shrift of any nylon.

Last, but not least, the spur-dog is also found over wrecks, often making its presence felt as it attacks a baited pirk. You have to bear in mind, however, that these fish, when they appear, can be so voracious and so seemingly limitless in quantity that nothing else gets the chance to go for your bait. When you consider that trawlers have netted shoals in excess of 20,000 individuals, you will start to get some idea of the problems which you are likely to encounter. However, there are also occasions when spur-dogs travel in fairly small shoals, perhaps consisting of only a dozen or so fish. In the first instance, repeatedly catching spur-dog can become monotonous and boring and it might simply be best to move to another wreck. In the second, if there is only the odd one or two and there doesn't seem to be much else about, then why not try for a few more? They do give a better account of themselves than the spotted dogfishes, running backwards and forwards as you bring them to the surface, and, once they have been killed and skinned, they do make quite tolerable eating. They don't, unfortunately, fight as hard as many other species, but they are quite interesting to catch in small numbers, especially if the sport is otherwise fairly dull.

To get the best out of them you might scale down to an outfit similar to the one suggested for bream, namely a baitcaster or light spinning rod matched to a small multiplier like the Ryobi T2. If you match these with a light pirk, replacing the treble with a double-hook rig as shown in the diagram opposite, then you will

SPUR-DOG: PIRK AND NATURAL BAIT

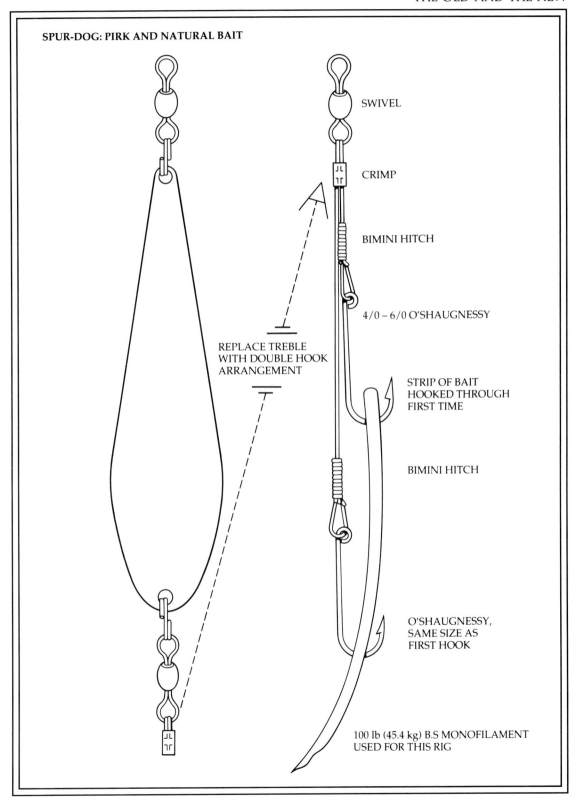

SWIVEL

CRIMP

BIMINI HITCH

4/0 – 6/0 O'SHAUGNESSY

REPLACE TREBLE
WITH DOUBLE HOOK
ARRANGEMENT

STRIP OF BAIT
HOOKED THROUGH
FIRST TIME

BIMINI HITCH

O'SHAUGNESSY,
SAME SIZE AS
FIRST HOOK

100 lb (45.4 kg) B.S MONOFILAMENT
USED FOR THIS RIG

almost certainly experience more than a few anxious moments as you bring any spur-dog to the surface.

Bait could be any type of small fish or sliver of the same, with two particularly successful offerings being either a long sliver of mackerel or a whole *calamari* squid. One thing you might find, however, especially in the second instance, is that the pirk starts to be taken by either pollack or ling, both of which are especially fond of whole squid presented in this manner. Get a big ling and you could easily lose the pirk, so it might be an idea to scale your tackle upwards to an outfit such as, for example, the DAM Megalite Uptide CR matched with a Ryobi Trymaster 70CL, a superb reel upon which I have landed some very big pollack. This outfit is still light enough to get a lot of enjoyment out of the spur-dog, but is sufficiently powerful to handle any pollack and the majority of ling.

When you do catch a spur-dog, you must take great care of the claw-like spikes which stick up at the front of each of the two dorsals. These are quite capable of inflicting a nasty injury, especially as the fish tends to writhe about and sometimes lashes out at the angler in its attempts to get away. The best thing to do is to immobilize the tail with one foot and put your other foot just behind its head, keeping well clear of the spines on the first dorsal. Stun the fish with a heavy blow to the snout and only then, when it is quiescent, attempt to remove your hook.

Spur-dog are actually quite tasty, especially to those people who used to like the similar flavour of 'rock-salmon' at the old fish-and-chip shops. They will, however, need to be skinned, a task which can be made quite a bit easier by nailing the head to a board, also the tail, and then working backwards from the snout. Make sure that you remove the spines with a knife and pliers, taking care not to cut yourself, since they do possess slightly venomous qualities.

All in all, the dogfish clan is not really a very exciting prospect, but there do seem to

be days when it is better to catch them than nothing at all. This is particularly true on inshore wrecks, which can sometimes produce surprisingly well one week and then appear barren of fish the next. However, if you fish in the simple manner described, then you will still have a good chance of catching other species. If you think about it from that point of view, then you can see that you are not really concentrating exclusively upon dogfish, you are more truly exploring what other species might be there to be found.

GURNARD

Another species which occasionally turns up when you are legering at anchor is the colourful gurnard, with its armour-plated head, sweeping pectoral fins with their peculiar three appendages at the bottom and its almost triangular spiny first dorsal fin. Coloration will obviously depend upon species, but grey gurnard, which are infrequent and too small to worry about, are well marked with light spots and have a reddish tint overall, even though the back and sides are invariably a shade of grey tainted by some other colour, such as purple or green. The head and lower sides are a variation of red or orange while the belly is invariably white.

Red gurnard, for which both tubfish yellow and grey gurnards are occasionally mistaken, are a much richer red than either of the other two species. They are also unmarked by spots and may be positively identified by looking closely at the lateral line, which is crossed by narrow, vertical plates. The pectoral fins, unlike the tubfish yellow gurnard, do not have a blue border. Overall, the red gurnard is, to my eye, quite a pretty fish, but it doesn't grow to any particular size, with a 2 lb (0·9 kg) fish being a very good one.

The tubfish yellow gurnard, which may be distinguished by the telling blue border on its pectoral fins and a lateral line which is a slightly elevated but otherwise fairly smooth ridge uncrossed by any plates, does grow to a big enough size to be interesting. These fish can be obliging when present, especially as where there is one there is usually more, and they have the added bonus of being very good to eat. A 10 lb (4·5 kg) fish is a definite possibility and may be best tried for with a flowing leger to a size 2 Aberdeen and a small, live sand-eel. Gurnard are decidedly partial to these and, provided that they are fished upon either the sand or shingle bank at the side of the wreck, will take them with enthusiasm. This applies equally to the red, but both species will also take prawns, razorfish and peeler crabs with gusto.

JOHN DORY

These weird and wonderful fish are more common in our waters than many people might suppose, often being found around wrecks in both deep and shallow water, although the numbers to be found inshore will depend to a large extent upon the water temperature. If this steadily rises, as in a period of warm, settled weather, then numbers inshore will increase. If, however, the summer months are marked by variable, unsettled weather, then nowhere near as many fish will penetrate to the shallower water.

To look at, the John Dory almost appears to be an upright-swimming flatfish. Its body is both deep and very compressed, while the head is large and armed with a mouth that can suddenly shoot out and trap other fish. There are two dorsal fins, so close as to be almost touching, and the first is armed with long, trailing spines. There are also two anal fins, the front one being armed with four conspicuous spines, although these are nowhere near the length of those to be found on the first dorsal. Pectoral fins are of only moderate size, but with a distinctive 'thumb-print' set just behind them on the body. The pelvic fins, which are set slightly in front of the pectorals, are long and trailing, and also armed with a single long spine.

If you ever get the chance to watch a John Dory hunt, then you will see how it seems to swim both slowly and very listlessly, almost keeling over on its side as it drifts upwards towards its intended prey. There is no sudden spurt of speed, no thrilling chase, just an inexorable advance in such a way that it might almost be mistaken for a piece of drifting weed. Then, suddenly, as a victim comes within reach, the mouth suddenly telescopes forward and traps it. The next second it has gone and again the fish is drifting listlessly forward.

Obviously, if you want to catch one of these fish, you have to use a tackle which will take advantage of the manner in which it hunts. To do this, the best way is to set up a paternoster rig with a long, homemade boom put together in the following way. First of all you need to slide a piece of plastic tubing over a nail and secure this in a vice or similar. Your next step is to take a length of stainless-steel wire and coil this tightly around the tubing for at least six turns, leaving it sticking out to a length of at least 10 in (250 mm). Turn the end of this and make an eye. Slide the plastic from the nail and trim it so that $\frac{1}{2}$ in (13 mm) protrudes both above and below the coils of wire.

If you look at the diagram on page 112, this should be made clear. In practice this boom is then set between two telephone-wire stops, approximately 6 in (150 mm) apart, and is stopped from sliding over them by a bead on either side. This leaves the arm jutting out, but still free to rotate about the main line if you are using a small fish as livebait. A space of some 36 in (900 mm) is left between the lower stop and the weight.

To work this tackle properly, it is essential to keep your line fairly tight, maintaining contact with your weight. Now this demands that either you fish in a very slack tide, which, incidentally, is the best time for John Dory, or you use a sufficiently heavy lead to hold its position. In either case you will be tethering your bait above the bottom and in such a location that a John Dory may assume its normal method of attack. That is what the tackle is designed to do, compared with

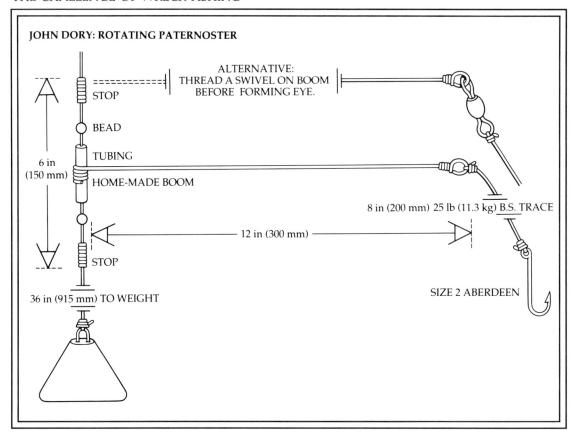

JOHN DORY: ROTATING PATERNOSTER

STOP

ALTERNATIVE:
THREAD A SWIVEL ON BOOM
BEFORE FORMING EYE.

BEAD

TUBING

6 in
(150 mm)

HOME-MADE BOOM

8 in (200 mm) 25 lb (11.3 kg) B.S. TRACE

12 in (300 mm)

STOP

36 in (915 mm) TO WEIGHT

SIZE 2 ABERDEEN

another which might expect a fish to go against its natural habits and will not work unless it just happens to open its mouth in the wrong place at the wrong time.

You could, of course, use a combined float and pennel rig, as described in Chapter 8, but you will find that the paternoster I have described, if baited with live sand-eels, is also attractive to both pollack and bass, while avoiding any conger. As a result you can use an uptider and smaller multiplier without worrying about their being ravaged by anything particularly gigantic.

Although, to be honest, I sometimes wonder whether, one day, it will take a very big angler-fish, especially as it presents the sand-eel in an ideal attack position for this species. It may not of course, but I just have the feeling that this is going to turn up

something special. I could be wrong, but on the other hand I do think that, if you give this method a fair trial, you could be quite pleasantly surprised.

TURBOT AND RAYS

Although turbot are not related to rays, I am nonetheless going to group them together as the same methods can be used to catch both types of fish. I will also mention the brill, a somewhat smaller flatfish than the turbot, which occasionally turns up on the sandbanks at the side of more southerly wrecks, particularly those to be found resting in less than 180 ft (55 m) of water. This can be immediately distinguished by the fact that there are no tubercles on the eyed side of the body — as there are on the turbot — and that smooth-edged scales can be found on both of its sides,

The author with a thornback ray, which accepted squid, taken on a wreck close inshore.

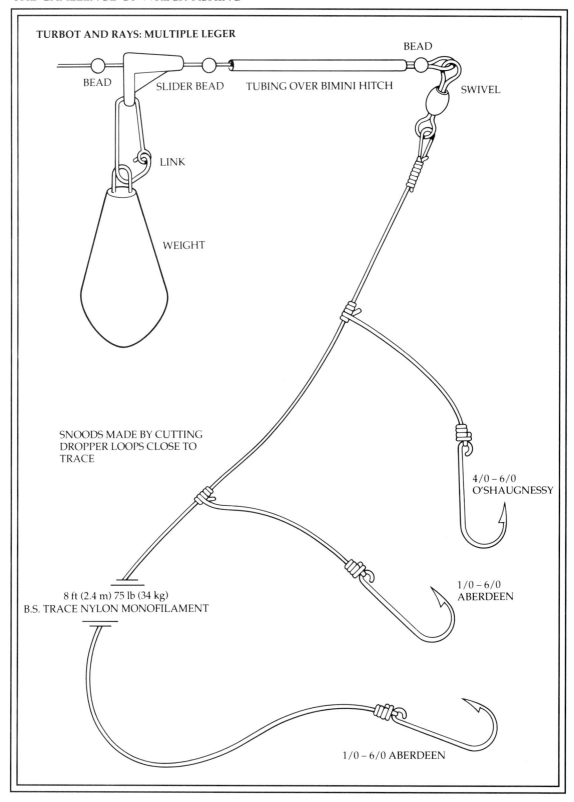

TURBOT AND RAYS: MULTIPLE LEGER

BEAD

SLIDER BEAD   TUBING OVER BIMINI HITCH   SWIVEL

BEAD

LINK

WEIGHT

SNOODS MADE BY CUTTING
DROPPER LOOPS CLOSE TO
TRACE

4/0 – 6/0
O'SHAUGNESSY

1/0 – 6/0
ABERDEEN

8 ft (2.4 m) 75 lb (34 kg)
B.S. TRACE NYLON MONOFILAMENT

1/0 – 6/0 ABERDEEN

a characteristic which its larger relation lacks. Its shape is also less broad, tending to a more diamond-like outline, reflected in its Latin name of *Scophthalmus rhombus*, whereas the greater size of the turbot led to it being designated *Scophthalmus maximus*.

Both species are active predators, feeding heavily upon smaller fish and often being encountered on live sand-eels fished upon a long, flowing trace. However, like most fish, they are opportunists and can be caught on a variety of fishbaits, especially when mounted upon the three-hook leger illustrated opposite. Fresh bait is best, but this can take a variety of forms including mackerel, herring, sprats and even strips of cuttlefish or squid.

The advantage of this tackle is that it will occasionally — so long as it is fished on the sandbank at the side of the wreck — take blonde, thornback or homelyn (spotted) rays. The last two, however, usually only appear on wrecks which have foundered in moderate to shallow water. On a few wrecks, all three may be found but in these cases the thornback can be distinguished by the large, prominent spines on the central portions of the wings (be careful of these, they can give you a nasty injury), the blonde by its light coloration and the smaller spots which go to the very edge of the wings, and the homelyn by the larger spots which stop well short of this point, seeming to have a clear border in between. The blonde ray also has ten or more symmetrically-arranged, round, pale patches on its back, these being bordered by a ring of small, dark spots. These patches are much more prominent than similar features upon the spotted ray.

All three species have a decided partiality for live sand-eels, but they will also take strips of mackerel or herring with enthusiasm. If both baits are fresh, then there will be little difference in their catch rates, but you will find that mackerel lasts longer on the hook and is much easier to get hold of. You can, however, on quite rare occasions, catch herring on a trace made up of six red flies, worked in a similar manner to conventional feathers. Frankly, this very much depends upon being in the right place at the right time and is not something upon which you should depend. However, just in case you do find yourself in the midst of a shoal of feeding herring, then it is probably a good idea to have made up just such a trace in advance. If you cannot get hold of either mackerel, herring or live sand-eels, then *calamari* squid will occasionally be successful and has the added bonus of being attractive to pollack, cod and ling. Baits of last resort would be sprats and defrosted sand-eels, these last having nowhere near the attraction that they hold when alive.

WHITING AND POUT

Catches of these species will depend upon the season, whiting showing at different times in different parts of the country. As for pout, well, I have yet to go on a wreck-fishing trip where someone didn't catch one. They may not have wanted to, but by golly they caught one, often two, three, four . . .

Catching either species is not very difficult. You simply bait a 2–2/0 Aberdeen with either lugworm, ragworm, peeler crab, sand-eels, mackerel strip, cuttle strip, squid strip, squid's head, prawns, whitebait, etc., etc. and then drop it down on a light leger or paternoster, wait for the series of tugs and strike. The result is a small fish with a look of goggle-eyed stupidity, a fairly deep body, barbel on its chin and vertical bands of darker coloration on its side. In other words — a pout, the whiting being somewhat slimmer and minus the bands and the barbel on its chin. Both species bite in a similar manner, but then fail to put up much of any kind of resistance as you winch them to the surface. You can, if you like, scale right down to the baitcaster suggested for bream, but even then only the whiting shows even the slightest inclination to fight, although from time to time a bigger fish will put an encouraging bend in the rod.

To many people, these species are the poor relations of wreck-fishing. The only positive

Whiting of this size are sometimes present in their thousands. Fish baits will often tempt the larger fish.

things you can really say about them are that they are very obliging and will often be present when little else appears to be. They are also edible, if somewhat unexciting, but are so easy to catch that there is little or no challenge involved in their capture.

BALLAN AND CUCKOO WRASSE

Although most anglers will concentrate on the much bigger ballan, I am nonetheless going to mention the cuckoo wrasse as it can be found in considerable quantities on a reasonable number of wrecks. It is more colourful than its heavier relation, from which it may also be distinguished by the fact that its body is neither as broad or as powerful. Both species have a formidable dental arrangement with an extra set of pharyngeal teeth ('pharyngeal' refers to the throat, which is where this extra set is positioned) which are rounded and designed for crushing such food as hard-backed crabs, limpets etc.

Despite this armature, it has become apparent over the years that cuckoo wrasse are more likely to accept lugworm than molluscs or crustaceans while the reverse applies to ballans, for whom either a peeler or hard-backed crab is an excellent bait. There is also a considerable difference in size, with the cuckoo unlikely to reach 3 lb (1·4 kg) in weight while the ballan has been recorded to double figures. Be that as it may, from various reports that divers have given to me, it has become apparent that potential record-breaking fish of both species are not only to be found upon wrecks, but are, indeed, not that unusual. I will not say that they are common, but they are certainly far from the rarity that many people might suppose.

Given the right conditions, I think it is entirely possible that a determined attempt upon wreck wrasse could see the record topple. This would, however, depend upon several different elements, namely the wind, the tides and strength of the current, allowing the skipper to anchor hard upon the wreck itself, which is the place where the biggest fish are to be found.

In this kind of environment, tackle losses are unavoidable. What you have to do, therefore, is to consider ways in which you can minimize those losses. A simple way is to fish an ordinary leger, but with the stainless link removed from the Ajusti slider and perhaps a loop of 16 lb (6·8 kg) breaking strain crimped to the weight. If this gets caught you can break the rest of the gear free, leaving only the lead behind. Another possibility is to tie a paternoster rig which incorporates a weak trace to the lead. The same logic applies to this as to the leger, but as an additional measure a float can be introduced to the tackle so that the bait rises well clear of the seabed, as illustrated on page 118. This takes the wrasse away from the cover into which it will immediately try to dive upon being hooked. You have a lot more chance to boat it than if you were to hook it in the midst of that cover.

The determining factor between success and failure will be the speed at which you strike and force the fish up and away from the shelter that it is trying so desperately to reach. To do that you need to fish with appropriate tackle. Now that doesn't mean extremely heavy gear, but it could well be that you might find an uptider to be a good compromise between lightness and power. Take, for example, the Shimano twin-power uptider. I like the heavier model for dealing with larger fish, but the lighter one may well be powerful enough to deal with wrasse, especially if it is matched with 25 lb (11·3 kg) breaking strain monofilament tied with a bimini hitch.

I know I keep mentioning this, but the fact is that a 25 lb (11·3 kg) line tied with a bimini hitch roughly equates to 35 lb (15·9 kg) tied with a conventional knot. Now the weaker strain line is thinner, allowing you to use a lighter lead as the tide cannot get such a hold upon the line. This makes the tackle easier and much more comfortable to fish. However, whatever you decide to do about the main line, make sure that you use a wire or nylon-covered wire trace. This is essential to prevent

WRASSE: BUOYANT PATERNOSTER

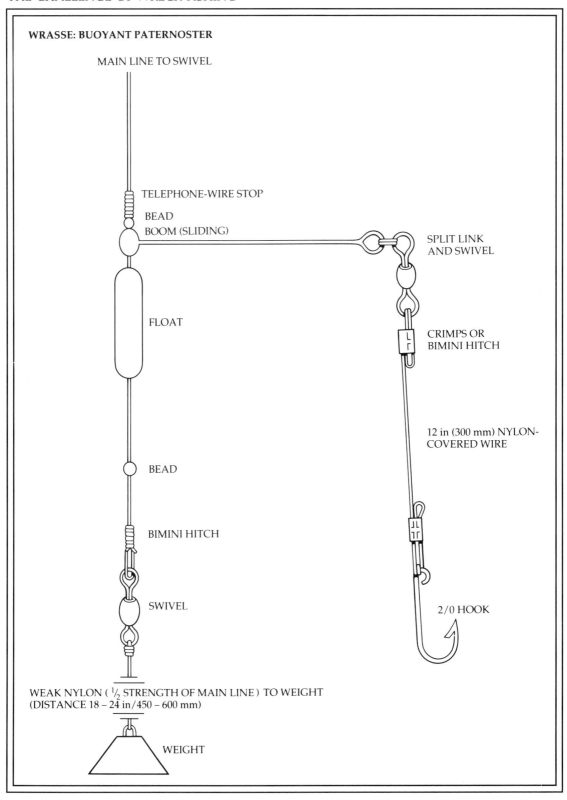

MAIN LINE TO SWIVEL

TELEPHONE-WIRE STOP

BEAD

BOOM (SLIDING)

SPLIT LINK
AND SWIVEL

FLOAT

CRIMPS OR
BIMINI HITCH

12 in (300 mm) NYLON-
COVERED WIRE

BEAD

BIMINI HITCH

SWIVEL

2/0 HOOK

WEAK NYLON (½ STRENGTH OF MAIN LINE) TO WEIGHT
(DISTANCE 18 – 24 in/450 – 600 mm)

WEIGHT

the fish from biting through it and securing its release.

One thing I would suggest, however, is that you take care, once you have taken the wrasse away from the bottom, to bring it fairly slowly to the top. Now the wrasse can, given a chance, be returned alive if you don't want to weigh it in for a record. This will, however, depend upon the speed with which it is brought to the surface and the depth from which it is brought. Wind it in quickly and it will almost certainly die, its swim-bladder unable to cope with the changes in pressure. Take it slowly and it has a chance, but don't give it that chance until you have brought it away from the immediate vicinity of the wreck. You never know, when you get it up you might find that it is only a few ounces off the British record. If you put it back, then at least it has a chance to survive. Give it a year or so, then pop back and see if you can renew its acquaintance. By that time it could have put on those valuable extra ounces.

But, to be honest, why kill it even then? Take an aerator and keep it alive until you have weighed it in, then you will not only have had the satisfaction of beating the best of British, but also the pleasure of seeing it swim away; that, I think will come to be the measure of a true sportsman.

CHAPTER ELEVEN

HINTS FOR DISABLED ANGLERS

Wreck fishing can be a very demanding business, imposing a lot of physical pressure upon the angler as he or she wrestles to get 'the big one' up and away from its home in umpteen feet of water. It taxes the angler's strength and coordination and places severe strain upon his back and arms, not to mention his legs if he is trying to keep his balance in the teeth of an imminent gale. It is so far removed from the notion of sitting peacefully by the water — that idyllic, somewhat boring picture that most non-anglers seem to have of our sport — as to make a complete nonsense of the idea.

So why do we do it? Partly, I think, because we like the idea of catching bigger fish than are normally picked up from the shore and because there is a certain reckless excitement about just dropping down into hundreds of feet of water and waiting for an unknown adversary to seize upon the bait. It is a means of escape, of getting out from the monotony of work, but, more than that, it is to do with the thrill of catching any type of fish, regardless of its edibility, or whether or not we return it alive to the water; it is also concerned with the angler's fascination, even his wonder, at what lies below the waves. It is for all of these reasons and more, but what I know, what I feel, is that fishing has its own very definite rewards, even though they may be as indefinable as they appear intangible to non-anglers. They are real and they are addictive, returning to us time and again as we seek to recapture the feeling of satisfaction that we experience at the moment when, despite the odds, we finally bring that 'big one' into the light of day.

I say 'despite the odds' deliberately, for the fish are in their natural environment while we are but fleeting visitors, daring to drop our gaudy lures into the immensity of a world which we can peer into, but never truly experience. Our tackle, ourselves, even the boat itself are mere specks, motes of dust upon a glittering horizon and yet, despite this, we still succeed, time and again, boating fish that live in our memory for years past the actual event.

And if the able-bodied feel such satisfaction at the moment of their success, then how much greater will be the feelings of an angler who has to overcome not only the obstacles which we all have to face, but also the disadvantages of his or her own disability. For though wreck-fishing can be hard, it is nonetheless an area where people with disabilities triumph repeatedly against odds that would daunt an able-bodied person. It is also, I think, an area in which they find pleasure in competing with the able-bodied on almost equal terms and, given the right equipment, succeeding with the best of them.

Take, for example, Ken Hatsell. Once an active fireman, his way of life changed dramatically when a brain tumour left him with very little movement in his legs. Did this stop him fishing? Not on your life. Instead he has gone afloat nearly every week for 18 years, building himself a reputation as a conger-angler *par excellence* with numbers of eels over 60 lb

Access is a major problem for many disabled anglers, resulting in all sorts of difficulties just to get on the boat.

(27·2 kg) to his credit, capped by three over 80 lb (36·3 kg)! He has also taken cod, pollack, ling, coalfish, to name but a few, and is such a familiar figure on the Paignton charter-boat *Tuonela* that locals refer to part of it as 'Ken's corner'.

And if you think that competition doesn't enter into it, well you are wrong. A large part of angling is concerned with competition, by which I am referring not to organized matches, but to the angler's personal quest for a fish bigger and better than the last one that he took. There is a certain amount of rivalry, I will not deny it, but if you are on board a boat and you listen, then you will soon discover that that rivalry is not directed at 'them' and 'us' but is concerned with a fellowship in which every angler celebrates each other's success, albeit sometimes couched in terms of rather rough and ready humour. And if an

angler feels a slight twinge of envy at the sight of another's personal triumph then, believe me, that is nothing compared to the encouragement which it gives him, providing concrete evidence that the fish really are there and the incentive to catch one just as large.

Obviously, physical strength will play a part in this. Ken, for example, has a lot of strength in his arms, but for people without that strength there are ways of getting around the problem and still catching fish. One way of doing this is to let the shoulders and back take more of the strain, which they can do by wearing a shoulder harness. Such harnesses are designed to take a lot of the pressure off the arms and to support the angler's back, taking much of the backache out of a hard day's fishing.

I persuaded Ken to try one for me, in this instance a Titan harness which had not been on the market for very long. He was really taken with it, finding it much more comfortable to fish with, even commenting that his back didn't ache nearly as much as it usually did after a trip.

If you look at the photograph on the right, you will see the harness which he wore, this being clipped firmly to the lugs of the Daiwa Sealine 400H that he was using. The harness shown, a Titan model retailing, at the time of writing, at £17.50, is lightweight, comfortable, and well-made, and an item which I would not hesitate to recommend. As it is usually only available through mail order, you will have to write to its designer — Tom Burness (at Titan Manufacturing, 8M, Falmouth Road, West Chirton South Industrial Estate, North Shields, NE29 8PF) — to find out the current price and the charge for postage and packing. It is a very useful piece of equipment, not only for people like Ken, but for anyone after bigger fish.

Another problem faced by disabled anglers, although a simple one, is not an easy one to overcome. That problem is access, where the disabled angler has to negotiate a series of slippery steps, get over the gunwhale and then find himself somewhere to sit. Alan Bingle of *Tuonela*, for example, made a wooden mounting block and keeps a plank handy for sliding over the steps and the block, so that Ken can get on board without too much difficulty. It is a much better arrangement than many, if not most, boats have to offer, but even then Alan needs the help of another person to get Ken safely to his seat. It would be nice if harbour authorities could come up with something constructive to help, instead of expecting boat-owners to take measures off their own backs, but at the moment nothing seems to be forthcoming.

However, even if the harbour-master cannot do anything about the design of his steps, you may well find that, when approached, he will still do his best to help you. Such help may take several forms, but a practical one is a permit which will allow you to bring your car to the top of the embarkation point for

The Titan harness in operation.

unloading your tackle. You will still need a companion to move the car afterwards, but at least you will not have to struggle as much as would otherwise be the case.

Another friend of mine, Charles Armstrong, who suffers from multiple sclerosis, finds exactly the same problem. He probably still has nightmares about the way his son, Christopher, and I virtually heave him over the gunwhale of one boat that we use. Still, for all that, his wheelchair, when aboard, enables him to fish any position on the boat in relative comfort, although it also presents him with a couple of minor difficulties to overcome. One of these is the fact that the rod butt slides on the canvas, making it awkward for him to put any leverage on the fish. To overcome this I designed a very simple piece of equipment which fits to a board cut to the size and shape of the wheelchair.

To the front of the board, in the middle, I bolted two L-shaped brackets. Now these tend to get knocked around, especially if you are trying to put a wheelchair into the boot of the car, so it is important for them to be made of sufficiently strong metal to withstand this sort of rough treatment. I then took a piece of aluminium tubing, big enough to take the rod butt and end cap, and drilled it close to one end, passing through both sides. I then slid it over a bolt between the brackets, securing one side first and then covering the bolt with plastic sleeving for protection. Obviously, the hole in the tube must be large enough to pass over the plastic and be free to rotate. All you do then is to secure the bolt to the second bracket and give the whole thing a coat of paint. Once that is done and you want to use it, then you simply slide the butt into the tube until it gets to the bolt. This then serves as an anchorage point and helps to take the weight of the rod. The diagram on page 124 should help to make this arrangement clear. It is best used in conjunction with a harness but is very cheap to manufacture. I made one for Charles that cost me under £3, although it would cost a bit extra if you bought some foam to make it a bit more comfortable to sit on.

Unlike Ken, Charles has only moderate strength in his arms. He can manage a smaller fish, but cannot cope with the struggles of a big conger. This took a little thought, but was eventually solved by getting hold of a Ryobi AD101SS Electric reel. With its power-assisted facility, Charles was finally able to break his duck and boat his first-ever conger (see Chapter 7). Anglers who suffer from the same problem could do much worse than to consider this reel. It might even be worth asking around to see whether any charter-skipper keeps such a reel on his boat expressly for this purpose.

So far, I have dealt with anglers suffering from problems with their arms and legs. However, one thing that saddens me is that I have yet to meet a blind angler, which is a pity, as there could be no insuperable difficulties for such an angler fishing from a chartered vessel. The skipper or his crew deal with the landing net or the gaff and they are usually only too happy to cut bait if you ask them. Now there might be a few problems making up your tackle, but if you are blind then it will pay you to teach yourself how to tie the simple blood knot (see Chapter 4). I know from my own experience, when fishing at night, that this particular knot is quite possible to tie just by touch, and I have even tied it with my eyes shut just to be sure that it could be done. For people with fingers sensitive enough to read Braille, I am sure it would not present too much of a problem and, once mastered, they would be able to make up any number of rigs. After that it is just dropping them down to the wreck and then settling back to feel for a bite, which is the same for the rest of us. When you get one, you strike and, provided that you hook it properly, you get it away from the bottom and then play it to the surface. Now the hard part is getting it away from the bottom in the first place. When you have done that and you have it moving, you can always tell when to stop by the reactions of the people around you. It is like the old joke about the short-sighted pilot, the tourist and the runway with tall trees at its end. The tourist, feeling a bit nervous about the flight ahead, approaches the pilot to find his eyes swimming murkily from behind a pair of pebble-rimmed glasses. After a moment's stupefaction, he manages to ask the pilot if he can even see the trees at the end of the runway. 'No', replies this individual quite calmly, provoking a near-heart attack for the tourist. 'But I always know when to take off.' 'How?' squeaks his audience, in considerable agitation. 'It's quite simple really. I just open her up to full throttle, then sit back and wait. When 635 voices go "Bloody Hell!" from behind me then I know that it's time to take off.'

In exactly the same way, the other anglers on board the boat will be curious about what is coming aboard. When you hear someone positively identifying whatever it is, then all

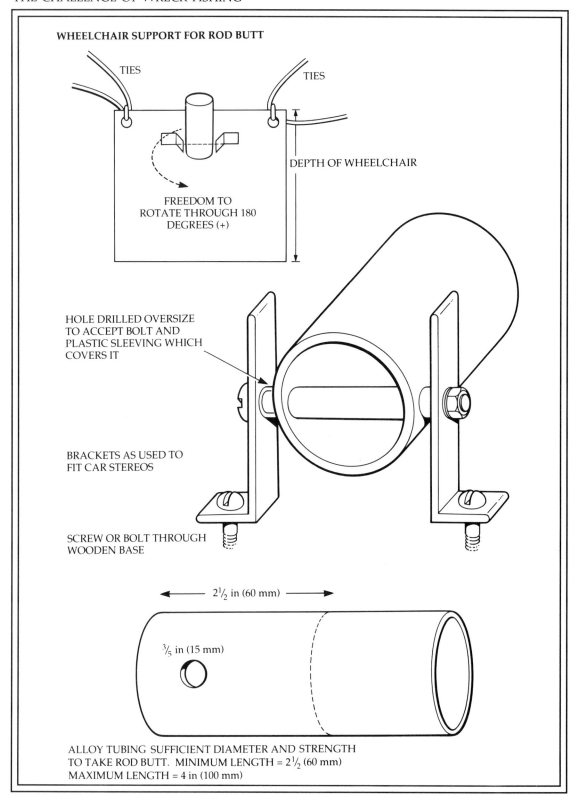

WHEELCHAIR SUPPORT FOR ROD BUTT

TIES

TIES

DEPTH OF WHEELCHAIR

FREEDOM TO
ROTATE THROUGH 180
DEGREES (+)

HOLE DRILLED OVERSIZE
TO ACCEPT BOLT AND
PLASTIC SLEEVING WHICH
COVERS IT

BRACKETS AS USED TO
FIT CAR STEREOS

SCREW OR BOLT THROUGH
WOODEN BASE

$2\frac{1}{2}$ in (60 mm)

$\frac{3}{5}$ in (15 mm)

ALLOY TUBING SUFFICIENT DIAMETER AND STRENGTH
TO TAKE ROD BUTT. MINIMUM LENGTH = $2\frac{1}{2}$ (60 mm)
MAXIMUM LENGTH = 4 in (100 mm)

Charles Armstrong waits for a bite, miles from anywhere, concerned with nothing but his fish.

you have to do is to give a last few turns, then stop and wait for the skipper or his crew to gaff or otherwise bring it aboard. Now I know that is oversimplifying, but I do know that if I lost my sight then I would want to do as much fishing as I could. Charter-boats, with their professional crew, would be an ideal way of continuing to fish.

Reading through this chapter, I am keenly aware of the fact that there are many things which I do, and take for granted, that would be difficult if not impossible for many other people. I have, quite obviously, only touched the surface of what is a much more demanding problem for them. However, it seems to me that the best way of dealing with any problems, at least those concerned with angling, is to get as many minds thinking about possible solutions as you can. A good way of doing that is to join a club, especially one which may have a charter-skipper or two amongst its membership. If you do, then you will nearly always find that there are people who are willing and able to help you, and that applies not only to the disabled, but to juniors, beginners and even the most experienced of anglers.

But then, to be honest, that is part of what angling is all about: fellowship, mutual interest, caring and a challenge answered in your own, individual fashion. In this instance, that challenge is concerned with wreck-fishing, but in the future it could be anywhere that your interest leads you to.

And, wherever that is, I hope there is good fishing.

INDEX

Page references in *italics* refer to illustrations.